Happy Birthday.
We are sorry it is late
Margaret thought it was
in November ———
    Margaret & I and many
others think you are an
    Intrepid Woman.
    George e Margaret.

PATRICK M.R. GIBSON

AN INTREPID WOMAN

THE ODYSSEY OF DOROTHY McLORN

Matador
9 De Montfort Mews
Leicester LE1 7FW, UK
Tel: (+44) 116 255 9311 / 9312
Email: books@troubador.co.uk
Web: www.troubador.co.uk/matador

ISBN 978 1848761 322

British Library Cataloguing in Publication Data.
A catalogue record for this book is available from the British Library.

Typeset in 11pt Palatino by Troubador Publishing Ltd, Leicester, UK

Matador is an imprint of Troubador Publishing Ltd

Dedicated to Dorothy's three children Majorie, Philip and Nancy

CONTENTS

~ INTRODUCTION ~

All her life, Dorothy was asked, 'Why were you born in Russia?' The immediate answer embraces not only her parents and her own birth in 1900 in St Petersburg, but the long history of St Petersburg itself, and its growth into a thriving mercantile centre where her family and many other English residents had established themselves in thriving businesses since the early eighteenth century.

The growth and history of the city were influenced by its geography. Dorothy was born on Vasilievsky Ostrof, one of the many little islands that are on both banks of the River Neva, which make up the delta; the Neva then flows 42 miles west into the Gulf of Finland and the Baltic Sea. The river is frozen for four to five months between November and April. During World War II, the German Army surrounded Leningrad, (as St Petersburg had been renamed), for twenty-nine months, from September 1941 until January 1944.

Where The River Neva flows into the Gulf of Finland, which is part of the Baltic Sea, the region is called Ingermanland; the Russians, Finns, Swedes and others who lived in the area fought over the region for centuries. The Swedes and the Novgorodians built fortifications in the vicinity. In 1143 the Swedes attacked the Novgorodians' fortifications on Lake Ladoga but were repulsed. In 1323, the Novgorodians increased the strength of their fort at the entrance of the Neva from Lake Ladoga, situated on the Island of Oreshek.

This island changed hands many times during the ensuing years until Peter the Great, Tsar Peter Alexeyevich Romanov, came to power in 1682; in 1702 he captured Oreshek, which was then named

Schusselburg, now Petrokrepost, the scene of many pleasant visits for Dorothy.

A year later, Peter the Great ordered the construction of another fort named Saints Peter and Paul, which was built on an island separated from Vasilievsky Ostrof Island by the Malaya Neva, where it meets the Bolshaya Neva.

St Petersburg was founded by Tsar Peter the Great in 1703 and called by Alexandr Pushkin a 'Window on Europe'. In 1702, Peter Alexeyevich Romanov issued an *ukaz*, decree, inviting thousands of Russians and other nationalities to help build St Petersburg. An Italian architect was put in charge and arrived in 1703. Not surprisingly the styles reflected the trends of German, Dutch and Italian architecture of the times. In 1712 a French architect by the name of J.B. Leblond introduced the Renaissance style and at the same time, Peter proclaimed St Petersburg the capital of the Russian Empire.

The St Petersburg of 1900, the year of Dorothy Raitt's birth, had been a thriving capital of Imperial Russia from 1712 and continued to be so until March 1918, after the Revolution. The city was renamed Petrograd in August 1914, again renamed in 1924 as Leningrad and yet again, St Petersburg, in 1991

In the St Petersburg Dorothy knew, on the other side of the River Neva to Vasilievsky Island, along the wide quays stood – and still stand – the Admiralty, the Winter Palace, the Hermitage and other fine buildings. On the principal streets like the Nevsky Prospect, were the best shops.

The most important streets and quays were paved with octagonal hardwood blocks about two inches thick instead of the usual cobblestones as in most parts of the town, so that the loud noise of horses' hooves and carriage wheels was lessened. Many years later, when Dorothy was in Tientsin, China, after a flood she noticed that some of the streets there had similar wooden blocks, which buckled, rose off the road and floated away, to be gathered up by the poor who dried them out and used them for fuel.

Architecturally, St Petersburg remains one of the most spectacular and beautiful cities in the world, with fine parks and quays along the River Neva and its canals. It has planned squares, wide avenues and straight streets with many gardens and parks which Dorothy often visited.

The government buildings were handsome, with columns and sculptures, and often painted in shades of yellow to pale orange with white, and pale green and white. The Russian government still favours these colours on the old government buildings; the modern ones are of steel, concrete and glass. At the end of every bridge there were small chapels usually with candles burning before the icons. Dorothy remembers them as being of pale-yellow brick with gilded onion domes. The waiting rooms of all the railway stations would have chapels, or if not a chapel, one wall would have icons, candelabra and religious paintings.

Dorothy's family was part of the growth of St Petersburg in the nineteenth century, including trade with Britain. From 1850 to 1870, St Petersburg imported more from Great Britain than from any other country, mainly coal, metal products and machinery. In turn, St Petersburg exported more of its products to Great Britain than to any other country, mainly rye, linseed, tallow and wood.

There had been a large English colony in St Petersburg for a hundred years consisting of business people, owners of businesses, ship owners, professional men, clergy, and of course diplomats. Most were well-to-do and kept several servants, a country house, travelled widely, and sent their children to England to school and college or university.

The history of Dorothy's own family relationship to St Petersburg dates back to the eighteenth century. Her connections there begin in 1769, when William Hubbard went to St Petersburg and established himself as a merchant. In November 1771, William Hubbard, as an English merchant doing business in Russia, was admitted into the Fellowship of the Russia Company. On his death, his two sons William and John carried on the business until 1806, interrupted by the Napoleonic Wars.

In 1816 John Hubbard recommenced the business and by 1842, the Petroffsky calico spinning mill of about 40,000 spindles was erected in the Alexandroffsky suburb of Petrograd on the banks of the River Neva. In 1851, weaving had been added to the spinning business, holding 1,200 looms, which continued all through the Crimean War.

In 1866, the Hubbard family purchased the derelict Schlusselburg Printing Works on the island of Schlusselburg, re-equipped it with modern machinery from Messrs Mather and Platt in England, and turned it into a printing works for clothes and all kinds of materials. In 1869, the Hubbard family purchase of the Spassky mill, employing 813 persons, adjacent to the Petroffsky mill, increased the total production of both sites to 84,000 spindles and 2,700 looms, giving an annual production of 24 million yards of calico per annum. The Anglo-Russian Cotton Factories Company was formed in 1897, by which time they were producing 40 million yards of printed material a year.

The Hubbards were a distinguished family. John Gellibrand Hubbard for example, who was born in 1805, became a Conservative member of Parliament, was a director of the Bank of England and raised to the peerage as Baron Addington in 1887.

As the century turned, in 1900, the year of Dorothy's birth, William MacCallum was the manager of the Schlusselburg calico spinning mill on the outskirts of St Petersburg. The mill was owned by The Russia Company and run by Egerton Hubbard, the second Baron Addington. William MacCallum and his wife had twelve children, three boys and nine girls.

One of the Macallum daughters, Louise Mary MacCallum, married Frederick Henry Raitt; the Raitts' daughter, Dorothy Raitt, was born in 1900. Another daughter, Margaret MacCallum, sister of Louise, married Edward Gibson; their daughter, Marjorie Gibson, died of cancer in 1915; there were also two sons, Edward Leslie Gibson, also born in 1900, and Humphrey Gibson.

In Dorothy's time, in St Petersburg, then known as Petrograd, there were four generations of the family: Dorothy's great-grandmother, Granny Henley, and her daughter, Granny Raitt, her grandmother, her parents, Louise and Frederick and her own generation, including her cousin, Edward Gibson, whom she saw frequently. The family were all British subjects.

Dorothy was a born into a well established and prosperous family, and in 1900, her life bid fair to be privileged and protected.

PART I

Russia
Growing Up

~ ONE ~
St Petersburg
1900—1905

I was not blasée; I was charmed

Dorothy McLorn, *Memoir*

Dorothy was born in a flat on Vasilievsky Ostrof, one of the islands that are part of St Petersburg. She was delivered by a midwife, a *babka*, at 10:10 p.m. on Saturday, June 16th, 1900. There was still sufficient daylight in the Russian summer evening for the midwife to see, and attend to her duties without the assistance of artificial light.

Her birth was coincidently heralded by sounds of summer revelry during the time of the year known as the 'White Nights', when the sun never really sets and over the city hangs an unnatural glow until it gradually dissolves into the morning light. Street lights are unnecessary. Dorothy was born at a time when everyone in St Petersburg celebrated; through the windows of her parents' flat on Vasilievsky Ostrof, drifted the sounds of people chatting, singing and romancing as they sailed up and down the rivers and canals on river steamers.

Dorothy was the child of well-connected and prosperous parents, and was well-connected on both sides of her family. When he was twenty-four, Dorothy's father, Frederick Henry Raitt, married Louisa Mary McCallum, whose father, William McCallum, was then Managing Director of the Schlusselburg Calico Printing Works. Dorothy's parent names could not be easily translated into Russian, but her own name was translated easily into Dorothea.

Despite their present prosperity, Dorothy's father's family had suffered early setbacks before she was born. When Frederick was old enough for school, his family had lost most of their money, so he and a brother and sister, both younger than he, rather than being sent to England to be educated, as was the custom among the English community, were taught in German and Russian schools in St Petersburg. They all spoke those languages fluently, as well as English, which was always spoken at home.

Dorothy's paternal grandfather, Frederick Alexander Raitt, was born near Sydney, Australia. His father, Charles Robert Raitt, Lt Col, was the last Governor of the convict colony there, she was told, but this has not been corroborated from records held by The State Library of New South Wales. Frederick Alexander was a midshipman in the British Navy during the Crimean War, and eventually settled in St Petersburg, where he lived for the greater part of his life, whilst spending some of the summers in Leamington, Hampshire. In St Petersburg, Frederick Alexander met and married Edith Mary Henley, Dorothy's well remembered 'Granny Henley', her great-grandmother.

Like most children in Russia, Dorothy had an old nurse, her *Nyanya*, whose name, Prascovia Mironovna, Dorothy still remembered when she came to write her Memoir. Her mother told her that her *Nyanya* would take baby Dorothy for walks in her carriage to join the other nannies and governesses, who watched their charges as they played amongst the trees in the 'prospects'; the trees in the 'prospects' were a playground for small children. The streets throughout St Petersburg are laid out in a grid: 'prospects' in one direction and numbered 'streets' in the other. The 'prospects' were wide, with a double avenue of trees down the middle, beneath which were wooden benches. A horse drawn train was started on Vasilievsky Island in 1860.

From this vantage point, one could admire the *mamki*, also walking their charges in their carriages, accompanied by maids or chaperones. A *mamki* was a wet nurse, a country woman hired to breastfeed a lady's baby. She was beautifully dressed. When she went out she wore a satin tunic or jumper embroidered in front all the way down to her ankles, in baby pink for a girl and for a boy, blue or some other pale colour, with a white lawn chemisette with long big puff sleeves. On her head was a crescent-shaped headdress called a *kakoshnik*, worked in beads with a veil at the back. This costume is based on women's court dress of the fifteenth century and was worn by the Russian court ladies for costume balls until the early 1900s. Around her neck, she wore rows of coloured beads tied with ribbon hanging down her back. In the winter she wore a pretty, full-skirted velvet coat, fur lined, the collar also edged with fur. They were pampered in their jobs which lasted about a year. On returning to her village, she was given a dozen of each of the undergarments and bed linen as well as the clothes worn while on her job.

Although Prascovia could not read nor write, she often told Dorothy the stories and poems, by Aleksandr Pushkin and others she had picked up in her previous place in a doctor's family, where the mother would read aloud to the children at bedtime. So *Nyanya* remembered them and repeated them to Dorothy.

A Little Bird

In alien lands I keep the body
Of ancient native rites and things:
I gladly free a little birdie
At celebration of the Spring.

I'm now free for consolation,
And thankful to almighty Lord:
At least, to one of his creations
I've given freedom in this world
From *Eugene Onegin*

When scarce a lad, his heart was captured –
A heart that had not felt a pang –
By little Olga, and, enraptured,
He watched her as she played and sang;
And one would find the children roaming
Together in the forest roaming.

Gentle Olga - in her dimple
One saw the cheerful morning smile;
Her sky-blue eyes, her cheeks like roses,
Her flaxen hair, her graceful poses
Her voice, were such as they portray.
From *Ruslan and Lyudmila*

I've been there too: I sipped some mead;
I saw the green oak by the sea;
I sat beneath it, while the cat,
That learned cat, told me his tales.
One of the tales I still recall,
And this I'll share now with you all…

Nyanya also knew other poems by Pushkin, such as 'I loved You Once'; 'The Night' and 'The Dream'.

Sometimes, her mother also read Dorothy other stories and poems, usually to put her to sleep.

Like other English-Russian families, the Raitts were able to spend their summers in the country. In the city of St Petersburg itself, the rivers were the scene of rejoicing as people sailed the rivers and canals. The first grand embankment on the river was known as the English Embankment and attracted nobles, the rich and the influential. At this time of the year it had an austere beauty and was the centre of attraction, with music and all sorts of sideshows. A curious feature of the English Embankment was that the entrance to the houses was from the River Neva so that there were no gates to these properties. In the winter, the English Embankment was the scene for the popular sports of ice skating and tobogganing, although by the time of the 1905 Revolution, the popularity of the English Embankment had started to decline.

Every autumn when the Raitt family came back from the country the double windows would be closed for the winter. Workmen would come to do this bringing fine sand, putty and white paint. Dorothy and her parents would bring pretty moss from the country so the sand would be packed between the outer and inner windows and covered over with the moss. The cracks would be filled with putty and painted over to look neat. Some of the neighbours put straw flowers on the moss. Over the front door there was a fanlight window, a *fortochka,* the centre of which could be opened for air. The French living in St Petersburg called them *'was ist das'.*

The St Petersburg winters lasted from November until March and were long, cold and dark. In contrast to the almost endless day of the Russian summer, the winter sun appeared after nine o'clock and set at about half past three in the afternoon. But despite the gloom, the backdrop in St Petersburg became a winter wonderland for Dorothy's childhood. Laplanders came with reindeer harnessed to little, light, low sledges and people would hire them to drive on the snow-covered ice: 'Father once took me when I was quite young; we drove along a frozen river and it was very exciting.'

Large public sleighs were used to transport people around town as they would glide comfortably over the snow-packed streets. Ice skating on the English Embankment and elsewhere, and tobogganing, were popular.

All through St Petersburg there are the Russian equivalents of the British pub or inn but in a much greater number; from these drinking halls, the clientèle stagger and collapse to the ground, only to be wakened during the winter months by the police, before they freeze to death. The Russian street policemen, *Gorodovoy,* are small, dignified, never smile, and have a very severe expression. They dress in long kaftans, wear large boots and a cap; they live in minute houses conveniently placed at the corner of each principal road. If anything goes wrong, they are never to be seen but appear as if by magic when the incident is over, dressed only in underwear, but soon puts on outer clothes. Their main duties consist of waking anyone who has fallen in the street, drunk, in frosty weather so that they do not freeze to death. The police hierarchy keep a record of every foreigner who lives in the country and woe betide them if they cause suspicion.

Dorothy remembers that when she was five, she was taken for a treat to Krestovsky Island. Here the Birzhevoy Bridge crosses over the Malaya Neva River to the island where they had built huge tobogganing slides about fifty feet high with a steep slope at the top tapering off for about a quarter of a mile. Dorothy was entranced watching but her mother would not allow her to go on the slide for fear she might get hurt. There were huge braziers near the *droshky* stands here and there in the streets at which people could warm themselves. The river froze over so hard that a small tram line was built running between a double row of small fir trees making a short cut across the River Neva to the central part of St Petersburg.

Winter brought many social events but by the end of May, the city started to come to life until mid-July, when, as soon as summer arrived, all those people who could would leave for the countryside. Only the Government and other important officials remained behind in St Petersburg. Most of them had a summer *Dacha*, a second home, on Petrovskiy Ostrof, and many were imposing buildings.

When the snow and ice had melted and it was sunny and lovely, the windows would be opened. The little children would be allowed to sit on the window sill to see and hear the organ grinder in the yard below and throw coppers wrapped in paper down to him.

After she had gone to bed, Dorothy remembers that she could hear the sound of the piano: 'Mother as well as friends and relations played the piano, but this was in the evening when children had gone to bed.' But there was much less music to be heard coming up from the river and through the windows of the family flat in those days than when Dorothy was born, due to the humiliating peace settlement concluding the 1904–1905 Russo-Japanese War. There were military parades, but not on Vasilievsky Island. Dorothy remembers being in a street doorway with her mother and grandfather; standing in their heavy winter coats between her and the street were a troop of mounted Cossack soldiers with sabres drawn, who were urging people to clear the street, using their horses and whips. 'But I didn't remember being frightened...'

However this revolution made little difference to the output of the mills belonging to the Hubbard family.

Since Dorothy and her parents lived a long cab, *droshky*, drive away from the side of St Petersburg where the English church was situated on the English quay, they did not attend the church regularly but, as Dorothy remembers, instead had Morning Prayer at home on Sunday without fail.

Dorothy's father read the Epistle and Gospel; the children read the Psalms for the day. When Dorothy learned to read she would read a verse in her turn. Then all knelt down and Dorothy's father read the Collects and prayers.

Until 1903, Dorothy's great-grandmother, known as Granny Henley, used to give huge parties at Christmas for all her many children and grandchildren with so many presents that each child had their own little table around an enormous Christmas tree decorated with nuts and oranges, followed by supper and a dance.

Children's parties may be much the same everywhere but Russian and German children's parties are an exception. Everyone is expected to entertain everyone else. So they all come prepared to recite, sing, dance or play an instrument to the best of their ability. After tea was over the children played games. Dorothy was told that in a certain doctor's family at the end of the party the hostess would call out, 'Well, children, go to it,' and they would dismantle the tree in no time, being allowed to take home whatever pleased them. An old nurse who had worked there said 'It was always a big tree and cost 300 roubles to decorate it each year.'

Among her earliest memories, Dorothy recalls that when she outgrew her pram, she was promoted to what was called a go-cart. It was high off the ground with yellow lacquered wooden slats like an armchair on wheels with a footrest and shafts. 'I don't know why but I didn't like it even though it was typically English.'

She also remembered being photographed at the age of three. She wore a pale-blue silk frock which she liked, edged with cream-coloured, narrow Valenciennes lace. Dorothy was placed on some red-carpeted steps and the photographer told her to watch the camera for a little bird, but there was no bird. Then she was seated in a different position and she would be sure to see the bird but was disappointed once again. This was the first time Dorothy remembers being cheated by a grown-up and never forgot it.

When Dorothy was older, she used to call on friends on their Saints Days. Calls were obligatory at Christmas, New Year's Day and at Easter. The gentlemen paid calls on the day of the holiday with large bouquets of flowers while the ladies stayed at home. The following day the roles were reversed when the ladies called and the gentlemen stayed at home.

Unimportant acquaintances were the last to be visited, perhaps on the third day of the holiday. On these occasions the long dining room tables groaned under the *zakuski*, the bottles of wine, and cakes, candies and especially the *pirog*, the pies, 30 inches long and 18 inches wide, one a fruit pie or tart and one filled with fish, or with a spicy meat filling, and baked quite whole,. The hostess sat at one end of the table dispensing tea or coffee. The guests sat and ate and drank her health, then went to the drawing room and new arrivals filled their places at the table. The party went on from about 2.30 p.m. to the early hours of the morning. Older guests played cards or talked while young ones danced if the party was being held in a large house.

Dorothy recalls that at one party a very elderly gentleman went into the garden and brought her a huge bouquet of pink apple blossoms: 'I was not blasée and was charmed by the gesture.'

In Dorothy's opinion, Russian food is wholesome. The poor ate very simply: cabbage soup, bread, and several kinds of cereal, including barley, millet and buckwheat. Wealthy families had French chefs and had wonderful meals while in the north, the middle classes ate more fats and starches (as in China), and more fruit and vegetables in the south of Russia. Breakfast in Moscow usually consisted of tea with cream, and in St Petersburg, of tea with lemon, along with bread and butter or sweet buns; occasionally there would be cheese or ham on the table. Dinner was a long, leisurely meal when all the family were together. A long table with a white cloth on which there were hors d'oevres or *zakuski*, followed by soup, sometimes served with cabbage or meat patties, fish, egg or carrot pie: 'simply delicious'. A roast followed with pickles or relishes. Vegetables were seldom eaten at dinner. Tea ended the meal. There was always bread on the table, white and rye. Servants always had the soup and bread and a cheaper cut of meat with barley, millet or *kasha*, buckwheat. Each servant received a certain amount of tea and sugar a month but were poorly paid.

'Butter week', *Maslenitsa* as it is known, commences ten days before Lent, and is a time of feasting when all Russia gorges itself with buttered pancakes about the size of a small saucer made from buckwheat flour; they are delicious served hot with butter and a little salt, and usually washed down with vodka.

Dorothy and her friends would sometimes be taken to a fair, a *balaga'nui*, which was held on one of the 'prospects' or quays or avenues. Everyone made a point of enjoying themselves before the strict observance of Lent when feasting stops until Easter Day. The Russians fasted religiously, especially the simpler folk. Parties and all weddings were forbidden. The English were quieter than the Russians; there were no dances of course, but sewing parties and Shakespeare readings were popular; people skated but were not supposed to be enjoying themselves. Ladies wore dark clothes and hats to church.

The ladies of the English community held 'sewing parties' all winter, when they made skirts, shirts, dresses, chemises, aprons and many other things for the poor. The scraps were sewn into patchwork quilts by Dorothy's great-grandmother and her maids. Great-grandmother Henley was always dressed in black with a white net cap with a black bow on her head. She had been left a widow, but one of her sons advised her badly with investments that lost her a major part of her fortune.

Dorothy's mother told her a story about Granny Henley. 'When she was quite a young woman a big parcel was left at the door addressed to her. It contained a beautiful opera cloak, a *sortie de bal*, of deep rose-coloured silk and wool material all lined with pale grey swansdown. She never found out who sent it. It was just gorgeous.' Later the current baby used to have it to go out in the pram. Dorothy was the last to use it as it was once loaned to a cousin who was going to be photographed and was never seen again.

From an upstairs window of the house where Dorothy lived on Vasilievsky Island, she could see the fortress walls of St Peter and St Paul Prison Fortress on the island of Zayachi. The prison is opposite the eastern tip of Vasilievsky Island called Strelka, which was originally built as a port. She could also glimpse the cathedral of the same name, where many of the Tsars are buried; the cathedral stands within the fortress walls and has a belfry almost 400 feet high.

From time to time some rather 'horrid-looking vases', knick-knacks and other small things, were brought to the Big House for sale. These objects were made by the prisoners in the fortress. The knick-knacks were made by the prisoners from black bread which was their staple food, chewed and moulded and dried. Although Dorothy and her friends knew the prison was there, they heard nothing about the prisoners since children were shielded from anything unpleasant. Dorothy was told that prison cells were flooded when the River Neva rose but so were all the low-lying districts in St Petersburg where the poor lived. Dorothy remembered the church bells tolling; cannons were fired which meant that the Neva was rising.

The circle of family and friends, and their as yet settled life in St Petersburg, undisturbed by revolution, was, as Dorothy grew older, broadened by visits by ferryboat of which she has vivid memories, to the neighbouring island of Schlusselburg, the site of her grandfather's factory, where her Aunt Margaret Gibson and her children, Dorothy's cousins, lived and who were to play a memorable part in her life in St Petersburg.

~ TWO ~
Schlusselburg

The hayloft was a lovely jumping-off place

Whereas the Island of Vasilievsky, where Dorothy lived with her parents, is situated at the western end of the River Neva where it joins the Gulf of Finland, the town of Schlusselburg, (now renamed Petrokrepost, meaning Key Fortress), home to her Aunt Margaret and her family, is built on low ground surrounded by marshes, on the island of Orekhovy at the eastern end of the Neva. The two islands are about 20 miles apart: Orekhovy is situated on Lake Ladoga at the head of the River Neva, east and upstream from Vasilievsky Island (Ostrof) where Lake Ladoga flows into the River Neva and ultimately into the Gulf of Finland. In order to visit her relatives there, Dorothy had to travel by ferry boat.

On the island is a cathedral, and opposite the town on a small island of its own stands the fortress of Schlusselburg, initially used for the defence of the northwest approaches to St Petersburg. The fortress was built in 1323 and used as a prison until 1928, when it was converted into a museum. Also on the Island itself is the Academy of Sciences and the Mining Academy.

But of most significance to Dorothy and her family is that the island was the site of the family-owned Schlusselburg Calico Printing Works. Dorothy records that the factory 'was built on an island on the River Neva where a wooden palace of Peter the Great's had once stood'.

In 1900, the principal method of transport between Vasilievsky and Schlusselburg was by twenty steam ferry boats, *yaliks*, which have high prows and are painted in bright colours. At this time, the Neva had very

Schlusselburg
Elise and Ellen posed before the Fortress Prison

few bridges; crossing from one side to the other was achieved in short hops by dozens of ferries which navigated the canals and rivers, letting the passengers off on the quayside landing stages at the same time as others boarded.

Both in Dorothy's time and in the present day, Schlusselburg could be described as the industrial part of St Petersburg; industry includes ship building, repair yards and in 1900, textile manufacture such as weaving, spinning, and the printing of calico; there were also woollen mills and other factories.

The first time Dorothy went to stay with her Aunt Margaret in Schlusselburg was also the first time she had been on a steam ferry boat. She was three years old and a self-possessed little girl with fair hair falling

Schlusselburg Calico Printing Works

down her back in ringlets. She and her mother were sitting on the port side of the boat toward the front and had a clear view during the journey. There was a mist which cleared in places and then returned as they progressed up the Neva. It was chilly and Dorothy kept close to her mother for warmth.

Near the end of the journey the fortress of Schlusselburg came looming through the mist. Dorothy was scared as she had never seen such a frightening-looking building; she clung hard to her mother who placed a comforting arm around her. It was here, after it had ceased to be used by the military, that many high-ranking people were imprisoned, including members of the Imperial family and also political prisoners.

When she used to stay at Aunt Margaret Gibson's in Schlusselburg, Dorothy shared her cousins' governess. She taught all subjects and the scriptures, the Prayer Book and so on, as her Aunt Margaret 'was not good at that' as she said herself. So Dorothy and the other children had to learn

Schlusselburg Print Works En Fête for Tsar's Brithday

each Sunday's collect '... by heart, to be repeated in our evening prayer for the next week and several verses of a psalm each morning besides some scripture reading'. This stood Dorothy in good stead when she went to boarding school; she was one of the very few little girls who could read the Bible aloud without difficulty.

In Schlusselburg, Aunt Margaret used to take Dorothy and her cousin for drives in the landau drawn by two fat horses, one of which was called Strawberry. The stables were big, dating from the days when riding-horses as well as carriage horses were kept. The coach house was big too, with a small carriage, the landau and several sledges. There were two coachmen, one of whom, Pavel, seemed 'really old' to Dorothy; his beard was going grey. He wore baggy velvet trousers, top boots and a coloured shirt with a belt. For driving he wore a uniform: thickly padded, dark-blue full skirted cloth coat, and a long sash wound round his waist. Watching him dress was great fun to the children but not for the coachman. The sash was wound up like a bandage and held by the other coachman or another helper while the coachman slowly turned until the whole sash was wound

Schlusselburg
L-R: Dorothy Raitt, Marjorie Gibson, Leslie Gibson and the toddler is Betty (Beach),
Daughter of John and Daisy

about his waist. His hair was cut in a bob and his hat, as Dorothy remembers, had a brim stiffly rolled and a soft crown. He wore a fur hat in the winter and also fur-trimmed coat and boots. This was the usual dress of a coachman or cab driver.

The coachman's uniform was characteristic of the Russian insistence on uniforms. Since the time of Peter the Great, Russians had been obliged to wear uniforms, beginning with the tiny first year schoolchildren, schoolboys and girls, university men and students, schoolmasters and all the various government servants i.e. civil servants and the armed forces. In the theatres and cinemas and at other functions, no officer seated himself until the curtain rose in case an officer of higher rank was still standing. Uniforms were always worn even when off duty and at home. In the hot weather or in the country, men occasionally wore Russian peasant shirts, sometimes embroidered and worn with a belt or sash outside the trousers. Peasants wore beards and their hair rather long and bushy all round. Their womenfolk wore shawls on their heads. Nevertheless, in Dorothy's home, the servants – who thought themselves a cut above the village women – wore black silk lace scarves and spoke scornfully of *shlyapki*, the little hats worn by shopgirls or governesses.

Dorothy remembers seeing beggars in the street every day: men, women and children. There were thousands of very poor people as well as hundreds of very rich. Many of the latter owned huge estates where they built model villages, schools, hospitals and factories which made articles for sale from the produce of the estates. Dorothy could remember jams, boiled fruit, candy called Monpensier and tinned meat, fish and vegetables.

There was a farm in Schlusselburg called Bellioff's which kept prize cattle from Switzerland and had a model sawmill, which Dorothy used to visit with friends. Dorothy's friends were twin girls of about her own age. They had a big brother of seventeen or so but Dorothy couldn't remember ever seeing him. Dorothy and the twins used to climb the stacks of boards from the sawmill and the hayloft 'a lovely jumping off place, high but soft to land on'. The two mothers used to have tea and chat in French; Mme.Vinogradoff was Swiss-French. The children however, spoke Russian together; Dorothy understood French but didn't speak it fluently when she was six or younger.

Sometimes, in the summer in Schlusselburg, a barge would tie up at their landing place on the River Neva, selling flower pots and rough glazed pottery for dairy and kitchen. They also had dolls' toys such as tiny dishes, pots and jugs costing about a penny each, but it took much begging on Dorothy's part and the twins to persuade Aunt Margaret to buy them some. In those days there was no such thing as pocket money.

There are two kinds of *droshky*, carriage. The first is most uncomfortable and consists of a flat board for the two people to sit on, with no back or sides, with wooden wheels and driven by an *Isvoschik* and pulled by a single horse. They tend to operate in the more rundown suburbs of St Petersburg which has miles of dreary streets. In the winter the *droshky* is replaced by sledges which also carry two people and are a lot more comfortable.

The other *droshky* is a well-upholstered vehicle for two, with rubber tyres, driven by a *Lihatch* dressed in a spotless kaftan and pulled by a beautifully kept horse.

As a child, Dorothy also travelled further afield than Schlusselburg. Dorothy's mother suffered from weak lungs and because two of her sisters, when very young, died of tuberculosis, she was very careful of her health and often spent months at a time in Lausanne, Switzerland with her parents, taking Dorothy with her on a number of occasions. Once when they returned, Dorothy's old Russian nurse had gone to a new job so Dorothy had a Finnish girl called Alma to look after her.

Alma had been trained by an English nanny when she was a nursemaid working for the Armstrongs, cousins of the Gibsons. 'Alma was an excellent person but rather serious.'

Her old Russian nurse had looked after Dorothy's canary; she also grew mustard and cress on felt strips on the windowsill and insisted on the weekly toy-mending time while Dorothy watched and listened to her stories. Alma did not talk much but she was very good to Dorothy.

The time came when Alma married an engine driver shortly after Dorothy, with her mother and Polia, left St Petersburg to go to Apsheronsk. Alma and her fiancé had met at the Finnish gymnastic classes, but delayed getting married for years until her services were no longer required. (Dorothy continued to correspond with Alma's daughter for years when living in Tientsin, but they lost contact with one another when Dorothy and her mother were interned by the Japanese during World War Two. Dorothy became godmother to Alma's son Alfred and daughter Aune.)

Dorothy could clearly remember the day in July 1904, when her cousin Joyce Burnand began to suffer from a pain in one leg. At the time, Dorothy and her mother had gone by train to Lachta, a summer resort not far from St Petersburg, to spend the day with Granny Raitt, Aunt Lilly and Joyce, Dorothy's beloved playmate, then five. It was a hot and sunny day and they all went for a walk to pick flowers. The grass was up to their knees as they picked daisies, cornflowers, buttercups and poppies. 'All of a sudden Joyce half stumbled, sank down on her knees and started to cry – her leg hurt so much.'

The others remained calm but Dorothy's mother worried about Joyce until she was taken to a doctor. The doctor said she was suffering from tuberculosis of the hip. Poor Joyce was taken to Windau, a children's

Schusselburg
McCallum Family House

Entire McCallum Family at Schusselburg
Back Row: Louise, Elise Jr, William Jr, Ellen, Alice
Middle Row: John, Margaret, Elise Snr, William Snr, Flossie, Edward
Front Row: Katie, Mary, Vera

sanatorium on the Baltic Sea, for three years, and was given every treatment available known at the time. At the end of this stay, the cure had been so spectacular that it was fully reported in the medical journals of the day. Before all this happened, Joyce had been using roller-skates and had fallen some time before the summer walk just described. Some people thought that the fall might have caused the illness so Dorothy was never allowed roller skates.

The settled life of Dorothy and her parents in St Petersburg, the family and friends, punctuated by the pleasant visits by ferry to Schlusselburg, came to an abrupt end in 1909, when Dorothy was still only nine years old. The shipping firm that her father inherited from his father came to an end due mainly to competition from Germany where it was not only cheaper but faster to deliver goods overland than by ship. Dorothy's father took up a position as office manager for the Maikop Oil Company and the family had to move to Apsheronsk, a small town on the Caspian Sea.

Dorothy's father moved to Apsheronsk before Dorothy and her mother followed. While waiting to join her husband in Apsheronsk, Dorothy's mother leased a flat on the second floor of an apartment block which was considered to be the kind of flat suitable for the aristocracy. It had seven rooms. *Nyanya* had looked after Dorothy until she was three years old, Alma had married, and so only Polia, their cook, remained as part of the family.

To take a lease on a flat was customary; at the beginning of the twentieth century, virtually everybody in St Petersburg either rented or leased the properties they lived in. A yard porter *Dvornik* (uneducated) was responsible for looking after the requirements of those living in the flats or houses which he served. He brought them wood for the fires and undertook many more manual jobs, also ensuring that their passports were kept up-to-date.

Preparatory to their move to Apsheronsk, Dorothy's mother now sold the flat, including the larger furniture. Smaller items would follow in due course. Dorothy went to stay with her Aunt Margaret Gibson in Schlusselburg during the packing.

They faced the prospect of a long and tiring journey to what was then the small village of Apsheronsk, unimportant, and consisting of one long street, ankle deep in dust or mud. Today it is marked on a map close to Baku on the Caspian Sea.

The time had arrived for the family to get ready to join Dorothy's father in Apsheronsk.

~ THREE ~
Journey To Apsheronsk
June 1909

Look, Mummy – deer!

From her early life Dorothy was not used to a long journey but the following was to become a foretaste of her married life.

After lunch, a comfortable droshky was ordered and Dorothy, her mother, Polia and the fox terrier climbed in; the driver clicked his tongue and the horse drawn carriage moved off. The horse went at a steady trot and as they proceeded along many of the prospects with their wide avenues of birch, elms or mountain ash and occasionally maple trees, Dorothy wondered if she would ever return to the city of her birth.

It was not long before they reached the Nevsky Prospect, the main avenue in St Petersburg, passing through the most historical part of the city, until they reached the Moskovski Railway Station.

Having paid the driver, Dorothy's mother carefully wrapped the fox terrier in some rugs she had brought for the journey so that the dog would not be banished to the luggage van. It was going to be a long, slow journey of about 6,250 miles as the crow flies from St Petersburg to Apsheronsk, and would take many days.

The Moskovski station from which Dorothy and her mother departed was built in 1851 and was the first of five other stations in St Petersburg and the one that served Moscow. In 1909, there were nine through trains each way between St Petersburg and Moscow. The line was known as the Nicholas Railway and was the prime Russian line, built to high standards; everything was a little better than any other line and a state-run railway.

The intermediate stations were often quite a distance from the nearest town because they were regarded as service stations, merely places to pick up more water, or to change engines if needed, or see to them in other ways, but not as a service to the passengers. The southern end of the line was Moscow's Leningradski Station.

The best service was Train No. 1 known as the 'Courier Service' which left St Petersburg at 22.30 hours arriving at Moscow at 10.00 the following day, with eight intermediate stops. There were no non-stop trains, nor could there be because of the need to change engines, which were coal burners. Their train was first class only, with an average speed of 35 mph.

The next best train was Fast No. 5, leaving at 20.00 hours and arriving at 08.45, which was first and second class. There were nine regular and three conditional stops, with supplementary fares for Wagon Lit sleepers. Other trains were considerably slower for second and third class. There was one day train in the summer known as 1c, which took almost 12 hours, but included a restaurant car.

In Russia, first-class carriages were painted dark blue, second class golden-yellow, third class green and fourth class grey, though there was seldom a fourth class offered. Wagon-Lits coaches were of varnished unpainted wood.

Dorothy's mother decided they would travel first class on the Fast No. 5 train, due to leave at 8 p.m. This meant they had time to kill so they strolled along the Nevsky Prospect admiring the shops while buying some tempting sandwiches for the journey. When the time arrived they boarded the train and found their compartment. It was comfortable and they had it to themselves. The train was long with many railway coaches. The journey to Moscow was 405 miles and took nearly thirteen hours. Dorothy, who had never before been on such a long train journey, spent the time looking excitedly out of the window until it became dark, when she eventually fell asleep. She awoke as the train pulled in to Moscow and by now the sun was up. Here they had to change and make their way to Kazanski Railway station where Dorothy's mother booked through to Novorossisk.

The next stage of the journey would take about 40 hours, allowing for the stops along the route, to cover the 920 miles to Novorossisk, the terminus on the Black Sea. It was now Friday and their train, the Black Sea Express, was due to leave at 7.50 p.m. With time on their hands they went for another walk, this time on the south side of Moscow, where they found a little café and ordered three drinks of hot chocolate.

The evening was drawing in when they boarded the train to Novorossisk (Novorossisyk), and by now Dorothy was getting fed up and hungry. Her mother had bought a selection of sandwiches while in Moscow and so Dorothy, her mother and Polia started dinner, or was it breakfast? It didn't seem to matter, they were all hungry. Every now and then the fox terrier was given a piece of sandwich which it eagerly devoured. Polia had brought bottled water for them all to drink as well as a small dish, which she filled with water and placed on the floor for the fox terrier. The train was comfortable and fairly empty, so they had plenty of room to spread themselves and once again they had the compartment to themselves. Whenever there was a sound of someone approaching, Dorothy's mother hastily picked up the dog and hid it amongst the rugs on her lap. It had been a tiring day so they were soon fast asleep, with the fox terrier buried within the folds of the rug.

They were now going south on the State Moscow-Kursk and Southern Railways as far as Rostov, where they would have to change on to the private Vladikvkaz Railway that operated south of Rostov. The Vladikvkaz line was an enterprising venture which opened up the north Caucasus for the production of wheat and created the successful port of Novorossisk through which the wheat could be exported. Being close to the Caucasian oil fields it could use the oil to fuel its locomotives.

The first stop on the way to Novorossisk was Tula, a town about 100 miles south of Moscow, situated on either side of the River Upa. Visited by Peter the Great in 1712, it soon became the largest centre for heavy industry in Eastern Europe; in a curious contrast, it was also pre-eminent in the manufacture of samovars. But Tula is probably best known as the birthplace of Leo Nikolaevich Tolstoy, born in 1828, one of the greatest of all novelists and the author of *War and Peace* and *Anna Karenina* among others.

Fortunately, as it was now June, the weather was pleasantly warm, but Tula suffers five months of frost in the winter. The train waited ten minutes while people got off and others got on. Dorothy woke up when the train stopped with a jerk, at around midnight, looked sleepily out of the window and decided she was pleased they were again on the move as she 'did not like Tula'.

From Tula, the gradient gently increased as the train chugged southwest up to what is now known as the Middle Russian Heights, a fertile plateau about 666 feet above sea level, to the town of Oryol (Orel). The town is situated on the Srednerus hills, 140 miles southwest from Tula. Here Dorothy, her mother and Polia alighted, not forgetting the fox terrier which had to be kept on a lead. It was now early morning so they took some refreshments in a small café. Dorothy's mother and Polia each had a *pirozhky*, a fried roll; Dorothy's mother had chicken in hers, while Polia had beef. Dorothy had a ham sandwich followed by a *ponchik*, a doughnut. They all drank fruit juices. Dorothy's mother bought more sandwiches from the railway café and, as they knew the train was stopping for half an hour, they all went for a short walk.

Dorothy was now enjoying the continuing journey, watching the corn swaying in the breeze as the train passed through the flat countryside. Their journey now took a southerly direction as it made its way to Kursk, a distance of 203 miles from Oryol. At first, Dorothy watched the changing countryside while eating her sandwiches and was entranced by the picturesque thatched houses and cherry orchards as they passed through Belgorod; when she began to feel sleepy, to keep herself awake, she started to make a fuss of their fox terrier.

They arrived at Kursk nearly eight hours later. Kursk *Oblast*, Region, is the main supplier of corn to the central provinces of Russia. Whereas Tula is situated on the northern slopes of the central Russian plateau of Sredne-Russkaya Vozvyshennost, Kursk is on the southern slope and is built on two hills, where many rivers and streams flow, and where there are huge iron deposits. Apart from corn, many other crops are grown in the area. It is also an important railway junction.

Kharkov, 130 miles down the line, would be the next stop on their way to the Black Sea where they would have completed half their journey. It was early evening when they arrived at Kharkov. Kharkov was to become the most important town in the Ukrainian Soviet Socialist Republic and the home of the Cossacks; an important railway and trade centre, in 1917, it became the capital of the Ukraine. The ancient churches of Pokrovsky and Uspensky are well known in the area and what was once the Catherine Palace is now the main part of the University, founded in 1805.

The train stopped for an hour so Dorothy, her mother, Polia and of course the fox terrier, found a little place to have a meal and to buy more sandwiches and fruit juices.

The train departed Kharkov at 7 p.m. By now it was dark, so Dorothy, her mother and Polia started to settle down for the night. During the night the journey took them through a small settlement called Nikitovka, well known for its botanical garden. Dorothy missed Nikitovka as she was fast asleep, dreaming of the time she would next see her father, who always seemed to be somewhere else in her life.

It was around five o'clock in the morning when the train reached Rostov, 274 miles further along their journey to the Black Sea. Dorothy was still fast asleep when the train juddered to a stop; she did not wake. Her mother told her she had opened an eye, turned over and went back to sleep while Polia continued to snore.

Fifteen minutes later the train started on the 154-mile stretch to Ekaterinodar, now Krasnodar. By nine o'clock, all three travellers were wide awake and eating the sandwiches which, since they had bought them in Kharkov, were by now rather dry and unpleasant. This did not deter Dorothy, who ate the rest of the sandwiches which her mother couldn't manage. At half past ten, the train drew in to Ekaterinodar and they knew they were getting near to their final destination of Novorossisk, as they could smell the sea. Here the train would remain for half an hour before the final 70 miles to the Black Sea. Dorothy's mother alighted from the train saying she would be back in five minutes. This was only an excuse as she had noticed a shop with toys in the window. A few minutes later she returned with a small parcel secreted within her coat.

Two and a half hours later, at 2 p.m., they pulled into Novorossisk. The journey had taken forty-one hours, including the time taken waiting at stations. Novorossisk is subject to the violent northwest wind, the Bora, which sweeps down from the Caucasus mountains

The next part of the journey meant taking a boat to Tuapse, a short journey of 75 miles along the northern coast of the Black Sea. The 'boat' was better described as a ferry plying its way backward and forward between the two ports. Having left the station, Dorothy, her mother and

Polia made their way toward the dockside and on the way Dorothy had a *morozhenoye*, an ice cream. They were early and found comfortable seats on the starboard side of the ship away from the wind, and next to a window, and waited. It was still very chilly so they kept their heavy coats buttoned up to the chin to keep warm. The ferry gradually became fuller as more and more passengers came aboard.

When everyone was finally aboard, the captain gave orders to weigh anchor and the ferry pulled away from the dockside. There was a strong breeze so Dorothy held on to her hat as she watched the bow waves ripple ever outward until they disappeared from sight. Occasionally they passed a ship going in the opposite direction, probably going to Novorossisk. The northern coast of the Black Sea always remained in sight as they followed it.

The journey to Tuapse, where almost everyone disembarked, took five hours. Tuapse is the Black Sea port for the Maikop oil fields which were discovered in 1900-1901 and linked by pipeline with the refineries at Ekaterinodar and thence to Tuapse. Tuapse was an unattractive, bustling town where Dorothy, her mother and Polia found a cheap hotel for the night. From here they were to travel by horse and carriage to their final destination.

They were up early the next morning, and after breakfast, Dorothy's mother went to find a carriage and horses for the journey. This was to be a problem as they would need to change horses more than once to give them a rest, and a fresh pair of horses would then be harnessed for the next part of the journey. The carriages themselves were much more robust than the droshkys they used in St Petersburg and they needed two horses to cope with the rough tracks and steep hills as there were no proper roads.

When all was ready, Dorothy, her mother, Polia and the dog climbed into the carriage and made themselves as comfortable as possible with Dorothy by a window so she could look out. The carriage driver looked wild and shaggy but was Russian. He spoke in a strange hesitant tongue which Dorothy's mother found virtually impossible to understand as it was so different from the dialect spoken in St Petersburg. Soon they were off at a gentle trot, glad to leave Tuapse behind them. The track climbed steadily upwards. The journey was to prove uncomfortable, hazardous and to take a long time.

The Caucasus Mountains stretch from the Black Sea to the Caspian Sea, about 625 miles, separating Europe from Asia. From Mount Elbrus, the highest summit in Europe, the range divides into two approximately parallel ridges. The northern ridge is broken into many mountain peaks and deep valleys while on the southern side the ridge is almost unbroken along its entire length.

Their journey was to be along the Russian or north side; the southern side is in Georgia. This meant travelling up the lower slopes of the mountains then down into the valleys. As it was summer, the weather during the daylight hours was pleasantly warm, but once the sun set, the temperature usually fell below freezing. The initial part of the journey was through a long valley where the forest was mostly of oak, beech, spruce, yew and hornbeam. Dorothy cried 'Look Mummy, deer!' as she saw the animals flee in all directions. An ibex looked from the cover of the trees as the carriage bumped along the track. A few minutes later they noticed a bear sharpening its claws on the trunk of a tree. Where there were signs of cultivation, they could see goats, and squirrels jumped from tree to tree.

The track now started to climb and became much narrower with a rushing stream far below on the left side of the carriage. Dorothy changed places with Polia so she could see out of the other window. She took one look and was terrified by the long drop to the stream below and thinking that the carriage would go over the edge at any minute, she closed her eyes and buried her head in her mother's lap. It took a few minutes before Dorothy dared to look again when she noticed fish trying to swim upstream. By now the evening was drawing in and the temperature dropping with a cold chill in the air. The horses looked exhausted and needed a rest. Before long they came to a hamlet and took a room in a hostel.

The next day they set off early with a fresh pair of horses and a different driver. There was a surprise in store for Dorothy, as they bumped along the track which in places was comparatively smooth but soon became stony once more as they were thrown this way and that. Slowly, Dorothy's mother put her hand into her large coat and withdrew a long, thin parcel. Turning to Dorothy she said 'Happy birthday.' Dorothy seemed at first to be taken aback; she had completely forgotten it was June 16th, her ninth birthday. Being bumped up and down in the carriage had put all other thoughts out of her mind. Hastily unwrapping the parcel, she found a small Russian doll about 10 inches tall which her mother had bought before leaving Ekaterinburg and which she had up to now concealed in her many layers of clothing. Dorothy's face lit up with a big smile and twinkling eyes; she was entranced by its pretty face, blue eyes and gorgeous clothes. The doll had a bisque head, soft body and was dressed in a traditional Russian costume in the *Kalinkavicki* style. She wore a multi-coloured skirt with an apron, had a large-sleeved blouse tight at the wrist and a black bodice with discreet embroidery. Her long blonde hair fell down her back and she had an open mouth and little white teeth. Dorothy threw her arms around her mother giving her a big hug and a kiss. 'Oh! Thank you so much,' she said. 'It's lovely and I shall treasure it all my life.' Dorothy's mother hid the doll carefully in a large pocket whenever they stopped to eat, or sleep at night, to make quite sure it was not lost or stolen.

During the journey to Apsheronsk, Dorothy, her mother and Polia stopped for refreshments in hamlets or villages and in the evening at hostels or when there was one, in a small hotel. Food was poor but her mother bought fresh fruit whenever she could which they all enjoyed. Bandits were not uncommon and travellers were sometimes robbed, so they were told. 'I seem to remember feeling deliciously scared and wishing I could remember all the wonders of this beautiful journey,' said Dorothy.

And so it was that Dorothy, her mother and Polia, not forgetting the fox terrier, finally arrived at Apsheronsk, which, as they were told before leaving St Petersburg, had indeed one long, dusty street. The house they were to live in was built of mud bricks and plaster and was not yet finally complete. The plaster was still damp but they settled in as soon as they arrived on 2nd July, 1909.

Dorothy's father, Frederick, had arrived in Apsheronsk a year earlier to take up his position as Office Manager of the Maikop Oil Company which was situated on the shores of the Caspian Sea and he lived there during the week, going home on Fridays to supervise the building of his new house. So at weekends, Frederick stayed in the house across the road with the family of the late Cossack Ataman, the head man of the district, who had two grown-up daughters and they owned and ran the chemist shop.

The oil fields were a day's ride away, but Dorothy, her mother and

Polia never rode over to see what they were like. Dorothy's uncle Edward McCallum was a mining engineer and lived at the oil fields while his wife and step-daughter spent most of their time in Apsheronsk. Their step-daughter, a girl named Jeanne, was Dorothy's only companion. The Maikop offices were based on the edge of the Caspian Sea where abandoned and rusting machinery stood in polluted, oil-soaked earth, not a blade of grass or a tree to be seen; it was an area of desolation apart from the up-and-down movement of the pumps extracting oil.

The people who lived in and around the area of Apsheronsk were very nervous of bandits. Heavy shutters covered every window at night and the Company Manager's wife slept with an armed Cossack guard outside her door at night. Whenever Dorothy and her mother went for a walk, to gather mushrooms for instance, in the open fields outside the village, they took a fierce half-wolf dog with them and a friend, Mr Macdonald, who lived nearby, for protection. Mr MacDonald was a very quiet man and seldom spoke. He had been in the Klondike gold rush and Dorothy felt he was very lonely and was glad to come along.

The winter of 1909 was now drawing in and while in this particular area of the country the weather was generally warm it suddenly started to snow. In fact it snowed and snowed and snowed and froze for weeks on end. Soon the snow had reached to the tops of the windows and a trench had to be dug all around the house for light and air and to enable a person to close the shutters at night. It was so very cold that Polia kept Dorothy in bed to keep warm.

Louisa Raitt, Dorothy's mother, now became very ill with what the young and frightened doctor believed may have been typhoid, but they never knew for certain. As she seemed to get no better, Dorothy's father was sent for and he reached Apsheronsk shortly before Christmas. Fortunately, Dorothy's mother survived in spite of the doctor.

During this bleak winter, many benighted travellers came and slept in a local cattle shed or hay loft. In the early morning they would come to ask if they could wash and have breakfast. Luckily Polia, who had been with Dorothy's parents for many years, was proud to take care of and feed any traveller. Dorothy paid no attention to these men and seldom saw them and neither did her mother. They just came, ate and went but sent gifts to the family at Christmas.

A young man who was to become a friend of the family was a member of the family of Bishop Colenso. Dorothy was now ten years old and Mr Colenso appeared to her as tall, fair, blue-eyed and very handsome. He was about twenty, an Oxford undergraduate and owned a beautiful bright-red motor car with a lot of brass trimmings and he even took Dorothy and her mother for a drive. As the roads were most uneven he drove slowly. but he did say the car could go sixty miles an hour! Mr Smith another young friend often called at the house. He, like Mr Colenso, was also tall but dark and on the slender side and not handsome, but he did not tease Dorothy so she thought him the nicer of the two.

In the summer days the highway robbers were a nuisance and were hunted like game. On 4th June, 1910, Mr Colenso, along with some friends, set out to hunt the bandits. He loaded his gun with all kinds of nails and bits and pieces of metal and propped it beside him on a horse drawn cart and off he drove. As Dorothy had already mentioned, the roads were poor and as the cart went over a bump, the gun went off into his leg.

Dorothy writes:

Mr Colenso was in hospital for weeks getting better but the leg, unknown to him, had to be amputated– so when he grumbled to the nurse 'My ankle itches,' she said to him 'It can't, you've lost your leg.' He was so shocked, he died there and then. This sounds like a tall story but mother, Polia and I felt so sad that I've never forgotten it. He was only twenty-two.

Dorothy, her mother and Polia lived in Apsheronsk for only two and a half years before her father was again transferred, this time to the Head Office in Ekaterinodar, or Krasnodar, as it is now called.

~ FOUR ~
Ekatinerinodar

'They had silver belts, daggers and sword hilts'

March 1914

In the winter of 1912, Dorothy's father received a letter from the head office of the Maikop Oil Company transferring him to Ekaterinodar, now known as Krasnodar.

Dorothy, her mother and Polia had lived in Apscheronsk for only two-and-a-half years and were now having to move again. Dorothy, didn't say so, but in a way she was pleased. She had only had the one real friend namely, Jeanne. There had of course been the very handsome Mr Colenso but he had been a bit of a 'show-off', and in any event, he had died. The only other man she saw from time to time was the slim, but not so handsome, Mr Smith, who was kind and did not tease her. She hoped that perhaps when they reached Ekaterinodar, she might find more friends and many things to do and to see.

The weather was very cold, nothing like as cold as it was in St Petersburg in the winter, but well below freezing. Together, they packed the household goods, furniture and all, which were placed on flat sleighs with straw to cushion the bumps. The family also travelled by sleigh, Dorothy's father and mother on a light cutter, while cook, the terrier and Dorothy rode in a rather deep box on runners. Polia being a peasant always slept on a feather bed with a mountain of pillows, which lined the sleigh. The household goods and furniture would follow in due course; because of the much heavier weight they would be far slower and would need to stop more frequently to rest the horses.

Ekaterinodar is the city where Dorothy's mother bought the doll as a birthday present for Dorothy two-and-a-half years earlier, and is about 760 miles due south of Moscow and 70 miles northeast of Novorossisyk, which meant that the journey would largely be the same as when they came to Apscheronsk, except in reverse: a journey of 660 miles.

It was now the end of January, 1913. On the return journey to Ekaterinodar, the family stopped at some of the small hotels where they had been previously. On this occasion, they would travel faster than before, as each sleigh was being pulled by three horses over snow. The drivers kept as far as possible to the lower tracks as the surface was flatter and less tiring for the horses. Adding to their increased speed of travel, no change of horses was necessary at the end of each day. The family and horses all rested so as to be fresh for an early start the next morning.

After travelling for two days, in the late evening they reached the town of Beslan, where they were offered hospitality at the house of a priest. On arrival, tea was served and they were made most welcome. Unfortunately, the priest and his wife had had a fire in their spare room the previous day where two beds and the bedclothes had been completely destroyed,. In spite of this calamity, Dorothy, her parents and Polia were provided with the best silk eiderdowns and pillows to sleep on, which had been stored in a cupboard and fortunately saved from the fire. 'Before retiring for the night we were given a comforting meal which was most generous of the priest and his wife'. The next day they were again treated to an excellent meal which was 'gratefully enjoyed'.

According to Dorothy, their stay with the priest was fortuitous:

> It was dark when we arrived the night before and were desperate to find accommodation. Luckily we saw a faint light in the window of a distant house which we approached and knocked at the gate in hope rather than expectation. The priest and his wife admitted they had initially been afraid to let us in for fear of robbers. But foreigners have generally been made welcome everywhere in Russia by peasants, rich or poor.

The priest and his wife would take no payment for their hospitality so Dorothy's father made a donation to the church. Their next stop was the town of Nal'cik which was an easy run of about twenty-five miles and where they stopped for a meal before proceeding on to Pjatigorst.

They arose late the next morning and although the road had a good surface, it was necessary to halt at a wayside inn for the night, before proceeding to Armavir, which is an important town about one hundred miles east of Ekaterinodar. A rich agricultural centre, Armavir is also noted for engineering and the production of boots and shoes. Here there was no difficulty in obtaining accommodation for the night, before setting off for their final stage to Ekaterinodar, via Kropotkin. On reaching Ekaterinodar the family stayed in a hotel for some weeks while waiting for the furniture and other luggage to arrive.

Ekaterinodar was founded in 1721; in 1723, the construction of the largest Russian ironworks commenced on the eastern slopes of the Ural Mountains by decree of Peter the Great. One of the founders of Ekaterinodar was Lieutenant General Willim de Gennin, a Dutchman who named it after the Empress Catherine 1, and the Great Martyr, Saint Catherine (*Ekaterina* in Russian), the patroness of mining.

In 1781, Empress Catherine II granted Ekaterinodar official status as a city. The Empress, who was born in 1729 in Poland, became known as Catherine the Great and ruled from 1763 to 1796. She was a legend in her own time and worked for the good of Russia. During her rule, the main highway across the Russian Empire went through the then young city of Ekaterinodar. From the west, the highway was called the Moscow Highway and from the east, the Great Siberian Highway. St Petersburg was known as the northern capital 'the window to Europe' while Ekaterinodar, the Ural capital, became known as the 'window to Asia', with Siberia and its riches to the east.

The town stands on the right bank of the River Kuban which is navigable for 142 miles from its mouth on the Sea of Asov, where it joins the Black Sea. In 1793, it was used by the Cossacks as a frontier post and became a military town. After the Caucasian wars were over it became a civilian town, and a centre for the region now known as Krasnodarsky Krai. According to the *Encyclopaedia Britannica* 'most of the area is a fertile plain. It has always been one of movement and of civilizations owing to its situation between the Black and the Caspian Seas. It formed a link between the Mediterranean civilizations which established trading colonies there; the Persian and Turkish empires of Asia Minor; the Mongolian and Tartar Steppe peoples and the Russians from the north-west were all attracted by its fertility and trading possibilities.'

In 1878, the railway station was built and during the 1890s, Ekaterinodar became an important industrial city for trade between northern Russia and the Mediterranean regions and so developed many industries, principally agricultural products, engineering and petroleum. The summer temperatures were warm with an average of 75°F while during the winter months, it remained below freezing most of the time.

Although Dorothy was not to remain in Ekaterinodar for long, there were a number of things that remained in her memory about the town:

> 'Open tram cars – which went to the end of the line where the open country began and then back again – the streets being swept with great branches of sweet mimosa – Street urchins selling tight bunches of lily-of-the-valley or violets. It was here that I saw peonies for the first time. Their scent brings this time back still.'

There were broad avenues and parks with birch, aspen, poplar and alder trees.

Dorothy also remembers the really gorgeous uniforms of the many Cossack regiments:

> I used to know which colour belonged to which regiment, all the way from white to black, yellow, red, blue, brown, magenta, sky-blue, and rose. They had silver belts, daggers and sword hilts and rows of silver cartridge cases on the breast. The tall fur hats worn at a jaunty angle, the high boots and really beautiful horses, all were a lovely sight at a church parade for instance.

The Cossacks are a proud people and this is demonstrated in their dancing which is imperious and very lively, their bearing and gestures are one of domination, to the accompaniment of the balalaika. They have never been anything but free men. The Emperor used them as his personal bodyguard. At the start of the Russian Revolution, the Cossacks were the last to surrender, and many of them emigrated. Every Cossack boy on reaching sixteen years of age would receive a horse, a saddle, a bridle and some land. But he had to be ready at a moment's notice to serve in the army. Dorothy could not remember if he got a pension as well, but he did get some education.

In days gone by, the Cossacks used to be sent to distant quarters of the Russian Empire as settlers. There was a group of them in Peking sent there by the Empress Catherine, either as traders or with her ambassador. In the two centuries which passed they intermarried with the Chinese. Their present descendants are indistinguishable from the native Chinese but until recent times had kept their Russian surnames and their orthodox faith. This applied until the 1930s.

During the summer, businesses and large shops were open from eight to eleven in the mornings, then closed, opening again from four to nine at night. In the evenings, people would gather in the town gardens to stroll about with friends or sit and listen to the band. Sunday was the day for horse races and on occasions, the Cossack Regiments would perform at a *dgigitovka* or gymkhana.

When all the furniture and belongings had finally arrived from Apscheronsk, Dorothy's father, who was now working at the main office of the Maikop Oil Company, and the family, moved to a comfortable flat on the second floor of a town house. There was no garden, so they all had to go for walks in a small park nearby. This garden surrounded a massive bronze statue of the Empress Catherine II, the city's namesake. Another reason why Dorothy remembered this place was: '...the innumerable primitive stone effigies from two to four feet high somewhat human in shape like the Easter Island figures on a small scale. There were no visible inscriptions and I never discovered what tribe had lived here before and had carved these figures perhaps a thousand years ago.'

(No record of these figures could be found in the history of Ekaterinodar. However, they might be among the earliest sculptures of numerous stone *babas*, life-sized female figures, that were erected by Turkic nomads between the 11th and 13th century).

Dorothy continues: 'These figures stood surrounded by very bright green grass which was rather tall, it was obviously not a lawn for in amongst the grass lived the most magnificent green lizards I have ever seen. They were at least a foot long and some three inches across the widest part of their body and of such a vivid green that it looked bluish and metallic.' Dorothy's fox terrier used to chase the lizards: 'When one was caught and bitten the flesh appeared very bright red and compact. But I do not remember noticing any blood.'

There was a time while Dorothy's family were in Ekaterinodar when they required an extra person to do the housework. Polia introduced a man who had asked her for work when she was shopping in the market. He seemed quite a decent person and very ordinary to look at. Dorothy remembers that he cleaned the rooms and served at table. One day he asked to speak privately to Dorothy's father, and it appeared that the man was an escaped political fugitive and that he had to leave as he had been observed by the police. Dorothy's parents supplied him with food and clothing for the journey and suggested he go and hide in Apscheronsk. Months later they got the news that he had arrived safely. He had told Polia that the family were touchingly innocent and trustful to have taken him at his word.

Dorothy and her mother were not destined to remain long in Ekaterinodar. Dorothy was growing up and her mother decided to take her to Switzerland to further her education. In Lausanne they stayed with Grandfather McCallum who had a large house. While there, during the summer of 1914, Dorothy was joined by her cousins Leslie and Marjorie Gibson, who arrived from Winchester College and Wycombe Abbey in England for their holidays.

While Dorothy and her mother were still in Switzerland at the commencement of the Great War, Dorothy's father left his job in the Maikop Oil Company and became the British Representative and General Manager for a subsidiary of the Lena Gold Fields Company, called the Sissert Mining Company. It was situated in a small town or large village called Sissert in the Ural Mountains and a far cry from Lausanne in Switzerland.

Because of the outbreak of war in 1914, the school Dorothy should have attended, failed, (for reasons unknown), so the following year, 1915, Dorothy's mother decided they should both return to Russia to join her husband.

The Russian Consul General in Geneva, Mr Yury Stravinsky, was a brother of the composer Igor: Fyodor Stravinsky, the father of Igor, died in 1902, and had four sons: Roman, who died in 1897; Yury died in 1941, Gury 1917 and Igor in 1971.

Yury Stravinsky told Dorothy's mother that it had been risky to travel in 1914, but now, a year later, it was much worse. However, the only route back to Russia that was open for them with the war now raging in Europe, was via England. Nevertheless, he supplied the visas and Dorothy and her mother left Switzerland for England on October 15th, 1915.

There was a submarine scare in the open Atlantic but it was only a scare. Having reached England without mishap, they took the train to Newcastle. Here there was a moment of panic as they were about to board a vessel bound for Bergen during a blackout; the British authorities rather doubted whether they were bona fide British subjects. Luckily, Dorothy's mother remembered she had her birth certificate in her purse, so all was well.

Dorothy was now fifteen years old and a teenager, tall with long blonde hair down to her waist and very attractive. She was artistic and enjoyed travel and meeting so many different peoples and races. On the voyage to Bergen in Norway, she was captivated by the red rocks and the beautiful fiords. The rail journey from Bergen across Norway, Sweden and Finland seemed to go in a flash, but she delighted in seeing the forests of evergreens and birches interspersed by many lakes. Finally, the train took them from the south of Finland, over the border into Russia and St Petersburg. It had been six years since Dorothy had left St Petersburg but was now back home again where she was born and in familiar surroundings; but not for long.

Dorothy and her mother stayed for a few days with her grandmother, Grannie Raitt. Joyce Burnand, she of the tubercular hip, came to visit so she and Dorothy played English patriotic songs on the gramophone, but the war seemed a long way off.

Unfortunately, all good things eventually come to an end. Dorothy and her mother prepared for the long train journey eastwards to the Ural Mountains and on to Ekaterinburg, a distance of 1,150 miles from St Petersburg as the crow flies.

The final lap of the journey was by troika to Sissert, now Sysert, a further 72 miles. Troikas are large heavy travelling carriages, drawn by three horses abreast and took three hours on good roads to reach Sissert. The Ural Mountains are a range of low hills rather than mountains but their importance lies in their being the natural frontier between Europe and Asia. Not far from where they would be living two streams flow side by side in the forest – one flowing toward the west and Europe – and the other to the east and eventually the Arctic Ocean. Dorothy had actually seen a signpost with one arm pointing west saying 'Europe', the other east saying 'Asia'.

~ FIVE ~

Sissert

Vast is our land and rich, but there is no order in it
1916

While Dorothy and her mother had been in Switzerland, Polia the cook remained with Dorothy's father when he moved to Sissert, or *Sysert*. The house was situated on a steep slope and dated 1742; it was built of brick and plaster and whitewashed. It had been the home of the Salomirskys, former landowners of the property and all the land around. The big house had twenty-two rooms, besides underground passages and cellars where Dorothy imagined the serfs had once lived. The walls were three feet thick. On one side of the house there was a garden with a lawn, flowerbeds, crab apple trees and sandy paths. An iron railing separated this part of the garden from the main square of the village with a big church in the centre. To the east there was a yard, with the stables, the coach house, cowshed and the chicken houses, as well as the house where the yard man and his family lived. On the south side of the house was a lake, with its dam, with the village on one side and great pine woods on the other three sides. Between the lake and the house there was grass, paths, bushes and Dorothy's father's hobby, the greenhouses. The rooms in the west end of the big house were not used by the family. Here there was a billiard room and what was presumed to be a ballroom with a round entrance hall from which a short passage led to the street door, which was never opened. However, the billiard room had large french windows which opened on to a big verandah with tables and benches, used by the family in the summer.

The garden itself was shady and cool in the summer, the grass full of wild columbines of every colour. On the lawn stood a big stone vase about eight feet high which held a variety of plants. This area was called the Lower Garden where the family would sit in hot weather, reading aloud and sewing. Beyond the yard, there was a big kitchen garden; the family grew all their own vegetables, both for themselves and their many servants.

The family employed a number of staff: Polia, the same cook who had been with them for fifteen years; Pacha, the parlour maid, came on from Ekaterinodar where she had worked with Dorothy's father; Anfisse, a local girl learning to be a maid, and Manya, Dvornick the yard man's daughter, who helped in the kitchen when needed. Nikolai and her father worked outside and looked after the stoves and fetched all the drinking water from the other end of the village where the well water was good. Old Alexei Dyedushka, who said he was eighty, was a good gardener. Alexei was a crafty old man who used to say to Dorothy's father that he 'should dig over that manure heap now' and so avoided the really heavy work. He lived in the tool shed. Then there was the coachman Feodor; for a while there was a boy to help him but he tormented the horses and was dismissed. Now and then during the summer, several extra people would be hired to weed the flower beds.

The Sissert Mining Company had government contracts for grenades in wartime as well as for pig iron, railway lines and many other things. Their mines produced iron, copper and coal. The gold and silver mines had been abandoned but coal was still to be found. There were charcoal burners in the forest. Many years ago, so the story goes, platinum, then an unknown metal in Siberia, was found in the gold mines but since it was not silver it was not considered to be precious. But as platinum was strong, it was used to make shot in order to shoot game birds. Malachite and other semi-precious stones had been found but that was long before Dorothy and her family arrived in Sissert.

The big house in Sissert was used as a guest house for the Works' Office staff travelling on business, or for government inspectors; there were always several rooms ready for visitors. Dorothy's father was frequently away on the firm's business in Ekaterinburg to discuss policy with the Russian General Manager and also to visit the other factories at Seversky and Polevskoy, all several hours' troika drive to reach, depending on the roads.

A troika is pulled by three horses; the middle one trots quickly while the outside ones gallop. Each stage is twenty-five miles. At every stage the horses were changed for fresh ones and the journeys took from four to six hours. Sometimes in the winter the temperature would fall to forty degrees below freezing point and for months on end would be minus ten to twenty degrees centigrade. A journey of two or three hours on a fine day with one change of horses, could take four to five hours on slippery or muddy roads.

The Russian General Manager lived 72 miles from Sissert in a handsome company house in Ekaterinodar with old Mr Solomirsky, whose family had owned the Sissert property before it was bought by the Lena Gold Fields Company. This manager, whose name was Mokronossoff, or 'Wet Nose' in English, was the son of a serf whose duty years ago had been the punishing or flogging of other serfs on the estate. Hence the people in Sissert hated him so much that he did not dare even to show himself in the district for fear of being beaten or killed. Dorothy's father was a great favourite of the two old gentlemen and would often be called up to town on 'urgent business', but it happened now and then the 'business' would turn out to be an evening of cards and tea.

There was a tale, possibly erroneous, that the Empress Anne, who reigned between 1730 until her death in 1740, had visited Sissert and had stayed at the house Dorothy and her family were now occupying. In commemoration of her visit she had presented a solid golden crown about seven feet in diameter for the dome of the Works' church instead of a second cross. There were four churches in Sissert all of whitewashed brick and plaster. The Work's church was richly furnished; the candelabra were solid silver, the icon-covers were also silver or gold, richly encrusted with pearls and precious stones. One painting in the Sacristy was by Raphael, brought from Italy by Mr Solomirsky in years gone by. The boys of the village were allowed to ring all the church bells to their heart's content at Easter and the noise deafened Dorothy and the family, who lived so near.

Sissert and some outlying villages numbered about ten thousand inhabitants, many of them descendants of convicts. Sissert was on the direct route that convicts, chained together, walked from Russia on their way to exile in Siberia, one hundred years earlier. Housewives used to run out with a bundle of food and thrust it hastily into the hands of the prisoners, then rush away so that the soldiers would not punish them. This was of course long before Dorothy lived in Sissert. It was now in 1915, a prosperous, well established community.

Here the men were well paid by the Company; each family owned their log house with a yard where they raised fowl and vegetables. Most people kept a cow or two and at least one horse. Food was cheap; steak one or two pennies a pound. Each householder received a grant of land from the Company for hay and growing grain, a different location every year. Fuel was free but the wood had to be cut by the men themselves. At harvest time the Works was partly closed to allow everyone three weeks for harvesting his crops and cutting firewood. The houses were clean and comfortable, rag rugs on sand floors, many copper pots and pans, and always a samovar.

A samovar is an urn with two handles and a spigot usually made of copper, or it may be of silver. The water is kept boiling in it by means of a tube down the centre filled with live charcoal. The water, when boiled, was poured into the teapot or teacups. Tea is never made in a samovar.

The Russian people love flowers, and there were flowers on the deep window sills: geraniums, calla lilies, primula, roses and ferns. The people were hospitable, kind and cheerful – until 1917. The up-to-date hospitals were run by the company in each Works, with medicines, a doctor, an assistant, nurses and staff, free to all workmen and their families. The schools up to grade 8 were also run by the Company. There were two girls' orphanages where the children were taught most lovely and intricate embroidery and lace-making. The Company provided them with food and fuel and they grew their own vegetables. The orphanage girls were popular brides, well brought up, and perhaps even with a small dowry provided by the Company.

When Dorothy and her mother first arrived in Sissert in 1915, they were a source of amusement to the natives who had never before seen foreigners, let alone their peculiar clothes. Leather-soled high felt boots were also thought to be queer, not to mention their summer dresses. Their dark leather gloves were said to be 'black skin', which really worried the locals.

Due to the war Dorothy's education had come to an abrupt end and as she was too young to be doing nothing, she read French and wrote letters to her many relatives; this was considered to be doing 'something'. However, she writes: 'I am glad to say that mother and I managed to persuade one of the village schoolteachers to come and give me a lesson in Russian every afternoon. At first my fellow pupil was Boris the son of the Works' Head Forester who was also starting to learn the three Rs'.

Dorothy thoroughly enjoyed her lessons and at the same time got to know a girl, four years older than herself, who became a great friend and companion.

'For a reading book I had a Child's History of Russia – and still remember the petition of the representative of Russian Elders in the 1300s on going to their more organised western neighbours, and telling them, "Vast is our land and rich, but there is no order in it ... Come and reign over us." One of these princes did so and became the first reigning prince or ruler of the Russian land.'

In 1915, most of the population had men in POW, Prisoner of War, camps in Europe, to whom they sent parcels or messages. Since they were unable to write even in Russian and none were able to write the German addresses; the names and addresses had to be printed in indelible pencil in both languages on the parcel, each sewn up in a thick cotton material. Dorothy and her mother did this for a long time; some parcels just held dried bread and Dorothy's mother used to write a letter and enclose a shirt. They kept lists of names and addresses. There seemed to be scores of families with identical surnames. This work used to take three or four hours every day.

In 1918, Grannie Raitt and Joyce Burnand came from Petrograd to stay with Dorothy and her parents for the summer. On most days, they all went for drives in the country. Dorothy sometimes went out alone to ride or to row on the lake in a heavy old boat. An American family who were good friends and lived nearby often accompanied Dorothy and family on picnics to the summer estate on the opposite side of the lake. They all climbed into a vehicle which looked like an Irish jaunting car, where six people sit back to back. The younger ones, which included Dorothy and her cousin Joyce Burnand, rode on horseback. When the picnic was over, all the women, including servants, used to go to the woods to gather wild strawberries, cranberries and mushrooms; the latter would be dried or salted for the winter. Grannie Raitt loved these expeditions and enjoyed her visit to the full.

In 1918, food and clothing were beginning to be hard to get in the big cities and towns but this was not a problem as yet in the Urals. 'I remember Joyce, before leaving for Petrograd, got a lining for a winter coat of well matched grey cat fur. We ate all the time. Food was ridiculously cheap when available but sometimes erratic.'

The house in which Dorothy and the family lived looked big, although it was only one storey surrounded by a big garden. None of the villagers had ever been inside so it had the reputation of being extraordinarily big and luxurious inside, which it was not. Nevertheless, shortly after the overthrow of the government, a Workman's deputation came to see the room the family referred to as the ballroom to see if it were larger than the theatre in the town so that they could use it for meetings. Luckily for the family, it was about a quarter the size of the theatre so the hopes of the deputation were dashed.

One of the wealthy local merchants in Sissert had asked Dorothy's father to keep his revolver for him 'because our house was much less likely to be searched...' This was in 1917. The gun lay for months in the top drawer of the writing table in the drawing room. 'I don't remember seeing any shells for it.' Then, one morning the maid announced a representative from the Works' Council had come to requisition arms. He turned out to be a small, very dirty man straight from the foundry, most polite; he had been told to go to every house and collect all the revolvers and guns. He stood at the door; Dorothy's mother proceeded to faint onto the chaise-longue, the maid waited, twisted her white apron and offered the man a chair which he scorned.

In an attempt to hide her fear, Dorothy turned her back and opened the drawer of the writing table; the gun lay there as usual – it looked heavy, big, and shiny – but it was not hers to hand over to the authorities. So with complete composure, Dorothy said, 'There is a small nickel-plated gun belonging to this house that is the Works', in the linen cupboard, I'll go and get it.' It looked new in its cardboard box, like a toy. She handed it over and got a receipt. Dorothy sighed with relief. The family never had any more searches, although they expected them daily.

As Dorothy lay in bed at nights she wondered about the future. She was now 18, and although the Russian Revolution of 1917 was in its early years, she had noticed the slowly changing attitude of many of the inhabitants of Sissert not just to her family but to each other. The younger people were becoming insolent and throwing their weight around. Respect for their elders was evaporating and they were quarrelling among themselves. Arguments started in the street between those who supported the 'Whites' and those who favoured the 'Reds'.

News travelled slowly to Sissert from Western Russia and it was difficult to separate fact from fiction. The incident of the gun had upset Dorothy and as she lay awake at nights, every unfamiliar little sound made her apprehensive and gave her a feeling of foreboding. Creaking floorboards made her sit up, and tiptoeing to the bedroom door, she would silently open it to peer outside, only to find there was no one there. It took Dorothy a long time to overcome her fear but as the days passed she became more confident and accepted the fact that the family would sooner or later have to move on.

Meanwhile, her father was very busy looking after the Sissert Mining Company.

~ SIX ~
Tragedy In Ekaterinburg

Kill him in the woods and be rid of him

April 1918

In January 1918 there began to be rumours of Civil War. At this time, Sissert, on the great highway to Siberia, was full of Bolshevist soldiers. Dorothy and her family were well aware of unrest among the inhabitants of the town.

The Constitution of 1918 set up by Lenin deprived the rich – the nobles, capitalists and priests – of their civil rights and of their supposed wealth; it guaranteed freedom to the working classes who had a huge numerical superiority. This caused uprisings throughout the whole of Eastern Europe from Finland in the north to the Black Sea in the south. A volunteer Army was started by General Alekseev, which was known as the 'Whites', and consisted mainly of Cossacks; opposing them were the 'Reds' or Bolsheviks, created by Lenin; their leaders were Stalin, Kamenev, Krestinsky and Trotsky, who took over military affairs in 1918. This was the start of the autocratic Soviet system and became the first Politburo elected by the Eighth Party Congress in 1919.

By May 1918, the Czechs, numbering about 30,000, had joined the Imperial Russian army during World War 1; still the best organised military force in Russia, they quarrelled with the Soviet authorities and joined the 'Whites'. They formed the Czechoslovak Corps in Russia from Prisoner of War Camps in Siberia and elsewhere, and together with Russian Imperial Officers and Cadets, formed the nucleus of an army in support of the 'Whites' against the Bolsheviks. When they reached the Volga, they were outnumbered and unable to proceed.

The fighting came nearer all the time. Young men and youths whom Dorothy knew, were there one day and gone the next, having been drafted, against their will, into the army as cavalry passed through the town, then sent to the front line without proper training or arms. There were frequent reports of artillery trains passing through Ekaterinburg.

'Workmen,' Dorothy writes, 'gradually took over the management of the Sissert Mining Company. Gradually, the heads of departments and my father as General Manager were all removed from their offices and their salaries remained unpaid.'

Shortages began to be serious. Sissert lacked grain for flour, oats and meal, the stocks having been taken over by the army. Dorothy's father hated to be idle and he interested himself in the Workman's Co-operative of which he was a member; for as long as it was possible, he used to go on journeys to find supplies of food, sometimes staying away for ten days at a time, travelling in a two-horse carriage in the summer and by sleigh in the winter. He slept in peasants' houses for there were no inns as in other countries. Money had become of less and less value, so at last he was forced to barter iron from the Works for grain or cattle. There was a small herd of forty-five first grade beef cattle, held by the co-operative by the time the family left Sissert.

In the meantime, deputations of workmen used to come to see Dorothy's father for advice. 'Everyone was polite and friendly,' Dorothy writes. 'Later, their attitude changed and instead of coming to see him and talk in the kitchen garden where he was often busy, a meeting would be called at ten o'clock at night, and my father would be escorted by six or eight armed men to see that he came to the theatre where he had to explain how to run the Works.'

10,000 men would be present. The first thing the local Soviet officials did after the October 1917 Revolution was to run the police out of Sissert so there was no one to keep order. A small group of men from the militia was called together by Dorothy's father to keep order, which he paid out of his own pocket until a government was organised and refunded him.

Under this new regime, all the family had to attend the dances and plays put on in the theatre, which were singularly unremarkable. The theatre itself was made from logs with a good stage and had been built many years before by the former owner, who put on private theatrical productions; later, it was used for cinema shows. No one in the country had ever seen or heard of the cinema before this. On the opening day, a movie was arranged for all the schoolchildren and their teachers, who were invited to come in free. The place was filled with hundreds of excited children who had solemnly marched in from all the schools near and far around Sissert, as none had ever seen a movie before.

During this time, most of the new administrators at the Works were released political or criminal prisoners from Siberian prisons. On one occasion, Dorothy was asked to dance by a young man. 'He was twenty-five and had a fine physique and good looks and could dance the folk dances better than I could. He invited me to dance with him again the next evening. However, he was killed in a nearby battle before the evening arrived; he had been in prison for murder, it seems.'

As the days went by, the local Soviet treated the more prosperous people in the village with severity, sending carts to carry away goods and provisions. It was possible to get permission to buy back at exorbitant prices prized possessions like furs and clothes. Curfew was at six in the evening.

A long branch of a tree was flung at Dorothy's horse by some women when a friend and Dorothy were returning home from a ride; no harm was done but, she writes, 'I did not want to be foolhardy and complain to the authorities'. Travel was forbidden without a special permit. By March 1918, walks and drives in the forest were no longer possible. Since the front garden was overlooked from the street, the family used it no longer. Later, in May all their horses were confiscated, but a kindly workman lent Dorothy an old horse to fetch drinking water and to cart away rubbish. The family did their best to keep out of sight for fear of being abused or even harmed. Every time Dorothy's father travelled away from home they were all very anxious in spite of the fact that he got on so well with all the local workmen who had great trust in him.

There was a time when paper money was exchanged from Imperial currency to the Kerensky rouble, only obtainable in notes of 20 and 40 roubles, which was not practical. Dorothy's father signed 500,000 roubles on slips of plain white paper in numerals 3, 5, or 10, which were nicknamed 'Raittovki' and which were actually hoarded by some people in preference to the government notes of the time; they were exchanged at the co-operative or the Works' office for Kerensky notes whenever required.

One day, eight armed sailors arrived in Sissert from the fleet in Kronštadt. They searched houses for arms, but they behaved well, as Dorothy remembers. However, she writes, 'The local Soviet was then instructed on how to behave towards the citizens and subjected them to the same treatment as in the French Revolution. My father used to have a commissar to accompany him on his journeys and my mother and I did not know if he went as a guard or a bodyguard'. To escape the company of such an official, she writes, 'Father once travelled with a merchant acquaintance to Ekaterinburg to call on the British Consul, starting at two in morning and staying at a Swiss friend's house till the Consulate opened.'

No one knew how long the family would be left alone and safe; from that time, the Workmen's meetings would often discuss the family, calling them 'bloodsuckers', their one topic being how best to dispose of them. A formal stamped and sealed notice tacked on the front door beneath a small Union Jack identified them as British subjects, but it must be remembered that an angry mob is not reasonable.

During the time that Dorothy's father was in office, the Co-operative had saved some capital and since the village had need of a saw mill, a flour mill and a new cinema, they would go some way to compensate for the prohibition of the sale of vodka. So these facilities were gradually built on some land that was for sale and proved to be very popular and profitable. Some Austrian prisoners of war, in the village since the Revolution, were no one's responsibility, so Dorothy's father found jobs for some of them, such as musicians; a violinist and a pianist who performed at the cinema. A bakery and a barber shop were started by the Co-operative and some of the men were trained to fulfil these jobs. A cobbler's shop employed some more. So they did receive a helping hand. The pianist used to garden for Dorothy's father every now and then when he felt he needed something more to do.

A Russian man, a semi-reformed alcoholic, in charge of the cinema who had been glad to get his job and was grateful to Dorothy's father for giving him the opportunity, told his mother what he had heard. One day, his mother came to the house and asked to speak secretly to Dorothy's mother; they went into the garden and walked up and down, talking all the time. This is what she had come to say: Her son had been in a tavern drinking and had heard some men plotting to waylay Dorothy's father (who was in Ekaterinburg on business) and to 'Kill him in the woods and be rid of him'. Dorothy and her mother would be dealt with later, as the local people liked him too much and were influenced by him, so it would be foolish to kill the whole family at the same time. As the telephone was not to be trusted, a cartload of potatoes was bought and the old woman started off for Ekaterinburg. If questioned, she would say she was going to sell some potatoes in town. She took a note to the British Consul from Dorothy's mother to tell him the problem and one to Dorothy's father telling him to remain in town as long as he could. This the old woman did, driving the 144 miles there and back, twenty miles a day on average.

After this, Dorothy's father stayed away, and the Commissars asked the servants why he did not return. The cook, who knew all about it, told them that a bad toothache and visits to a dentist had delayed him. Then their cook, Polia applied for a permit for Dorothy and her mother to go to Ekaterinburg.

Ten days later at four o'clock one morning, poorly dressed, shawls on their heads, their luggage in flour sacks, and helped by a Russian woman friend who found a driver, a semi-idiot, for them and a team of horses, they left home and drove to the house of Swiss friends in Ekaterinburg. The friends had moved from town for the summer and were living in a country villa by Lake Iset, surrounded by a pine forest about twelve miles outside Ekaterinburg. Dorothy and her mother joined them. Their father was there already.

'Father used to sit in a rowing boat most of the day with a fishing rod, pretending to fish on the lake.' He had been lent an old rod by his Swiss friend; occasionally baited the hook and cast the line as far as he could. Dorothy's father was not really interested in fishing but he had to do something and went through the motions in case anyone was watching from the shore. Sometimes he had a bite and reeled in his catch but did not know what to do with it until it had stopped jumping about in the bottom of the boat when he could remove the hook. Fish did make a pleasant addition to their menu. The water was crystal clear and he enjoyed observing perch and pike swimming around the boat. Often he simply watched a drop of water fall from the line creating an ever-enlarging ripple on the surface of the lake.

It was also a time to contemplate the future. One thing was certain: news of the Revolution and its progress was sporadic and usually wrong. The only reliable information was when fighting was almost upon them. Would they be able to return to their home in Sissert or had the time arrived for them to flee eastward? Going west was out of the question. Time would tell.

Many British did the same by hiding in the same way while they were being hunted, only coming ashore to sleep in their house. Most peculiarly, searches were never made at night time. The women spent their days walking about the woods, ostensibly gathering mushrooms like any of the summer visitors. They watched bands of men entering houses, confiscating food and clothes. A party of 'hunted' men, but never the same group, would wander into town on a daily basis to buy the paper, listen to rumours and probably to buy stores as well. Dorothy and her parents spent six weeks with these friends.

News came that the Czech and White Russian troops were advancing. The Emperor Nicholas II and the Imperial family, who had arrived by train in Ekaterinodar on 30th April 1918, were imprisoned for eleven weeks in 49 Voznesensky Prospekt, known as Ipatiev House, next door to the house occupied by Mr Solomirsky.

One evening, when almost dark, Dorothy, her mother and the wife of their Swiss friends, decided to visit Ekaterinburg. It was thought too dangerous for the men to visit at night in case they were mistaken for 'Whites' and shot. The Swiss lady had an old car; there was no proper road, so they drove along the track to the outskirts of Ekaterinburg and left the car with a friend whom the Swiss couple had known for years. Making their way along the back streets, they arrived at Voznesensky Prospekt. It was a warm, moonlit night with only the occasional cloud visible, and many people were out, some hurrying along the street, while others whispered together in small groups. There was a feeling of unease, of foreboding. Dorothy soon realised that the chatter was all about the Tsar Nicholas II and his family.

As they wandered along Voznesensky Prospekt, they came to Ipatiev House, a large two-storey building, lit up on every side and surrounded by scaffolding and boards that reached the roof. There were armed guards everywhere: on the street; on the scaffolding and even on the roof.

Dorothy recognised a number of the guards who were citizens of Sissert and whom she knew by sight. When Dorothy and her friends stopped to look at the house, they were told to move along immediately and not to linger. They returned home by a roundabout route to avoid raising suspicion.

On his return home, one man from Sissert claimed that he had seen all the Imperial Family shot to death in Ekaterinburg. This turned out to be true as Tsar Nicholas II and his family were killed on the night of July 16-17 in 1918. Ironically, the White Russians and their Czech allies entered Ekaterinburg on 25th July and took over the town, driving out the 'Reds', but it was too late to save the lives of Tsar Nicholas II and his family.

At this time, many prominent men of Ekakerinburg had been arrested and kept in the Hotel Amerika. There was a daily roll call. From time to time, some were taken out and forced to walk wearing only one shoe, outside the town, where they were shot in or near shallow trenches. Most common people were ignorant of what was going on and were easily led by agitators. Perhaps because Dorothy and her parents were foreign, or because her father was popular with the men, 'A great many women came to see my mother to ask advice or to beg for coffins from the Company at the time of reprisals and executions. The front hall was often full of people come to ask for help or advice.'

Although Dorothy and her family remained in Ekaterinburg, the Spanish influenza 'struck their house in Sissert' and later the whole village suffered. Dorothy's father was lucky enough to get a trained nurse in to help for a short while. The elderly doctor took his family and fled the district; his assistant, called a 'Feldsher', coped all alone in a district of about 10,000 people. He was also a hero during a typhus epidemic. As there was a great lack of medical supplies due to the war, Dorothy's father gave the hospital all the supplies the family possessed from their own medicine chest, which was said to have saved many lives.

The new anti-revolutionary regime, White Russians, now in Sissert, began to search for Bolshevik ringleaders, some of whom were shot. There was much cruelty on both sides. At some point in 1918, the Bolshevik Government left the village leaving no one in charge. The influential people of the whole district held a meeting at which it was proposed that a Committee of Public Safety be organised.

'As there were no public funds available, my father paid the militia men out of his own pocket until things got organised,' Dorothy writes. Then it was solemnly suggested by the Committee that Dorothy's father be elected 'Ruler of the district with a constitution as in England where everything runs smoothly'. However, as Dorothy's father told them, he was British, not Russian, and could not take any part in a local government, but he was touched by their faith in him in spite of the differences in nationality, creed and outlook. Despite the continual threat of famine Dorothy's family were promised food by some of the friendly merchants.

The drama and fear of the three years of 1917, 1918 and 1919 may have confused Dorothy's memory and did not really remember in what order events occurred. The murder of Emperor Nicholas II had been brought forward while the White Army, the anti-Bolsheviks led by General M. Alekseev, advanced from the East and the Red Army, the Bolsheviks, led by Trotsky, retreated to the West.

Dorothy's family's Swiss friends had arranged, in case of need, while the Bolsheviks were still holding Ekaterinburg, to hide the family in huge beer vats of the brewery where Mr Fischer was brew master and manager. The 'Whites', the loyal Russian troops consisting largely of Cossacks, seemed quite definitely to have the upper hand by now with the 'Reds' driven out. There were many funerals every day as people searched the shallow graves and found bodies of executed relatives among the dead. The coffins were just pine planks loosely nailed together. Mr Mokronossoff's body was found among those who had been killed.

It was now safe for Dorothy and her parents to return home to Sissert. They set off in four troikas with their Swiss hosts now to be their guests. The servants were delighted to welcome the family home again. Apparently while away in Ekaterinburg, 'White' officers had occupied the house in Sissert, behaving very well, not even using the provisions left behind, while the yard had sheltered over a hundred people with cattle and horses. During the fighting nearby, a shell burst in the garden, but no one was hurt; the only victim was a pet pure bred Orpington cock. Dorothy's father arranged for the servants to bury all silverware in part of the tumbledown cellars. As far as Dorothy knew, these instructions were carried out, but they never saw any of it again. Probably it was used to buy food and shelter during the hard times that followed.

The 'Red' Army, created in January 1918, started to turn the tables on the 'Whites' when Trotsky managed to rally his troops. This resulted in villages and regions repeatedly changing hands with appalling atrocities carried out by both sides. There was friction between the Czech Generals and the White Russian officers, Denikin and Kolchak; military blunders ensued which was an advantage to the Reds. Small detachments of British troops were stationed in various places throughout Russia to support the White Army, for in those days the public assumed that the Red uprising would sooner or later be stamped out, and the Provisional Government of Kerensky, Whites, would take over. There were even small British armed naval vessels *HMS Kent* and *HMS Suffolk* at that time lying in Vladivostok harbour. In the meantime, British officers were kept busy drilling Russian troops.

Dorothy's father invited several officers to come to Sissert for a weekend but before this happened, the British Army in Ekaterinburg were suddenly recalled. There was a grand farewell concert in the theatre in Ekaterinburg with songs and skits and a band. It was all most impressive but the family in Sissert felt terribly let down. Most foreign troops were recalled from Russia and Siberia while this was still possible, with a few remaining to guard the Trans-Siberian Railway. By now the Russians on the whole were optimistic that the Revolution would soon be over.

Fully aware that the Bolsheviks were now gaining the upper hand and that British military support had been recalled, Dorothy and the family realised only too well the invidious position they were left in, especially as the British forces had sided with the Whites. During the months that followed, Dorothy and the rest of the household kept a low profile, not wishing to draw attention to themselves or their Swiss friends. In the full knowledge that he was vulnerable and could be killed at any time, Dorothy's father nevertheless continued to help the people of Sissert as far as he was able. It is a measure of their respect for him that the locals appreciated his position and what he was trying to do to help his comrades and other inhabitants of Sissert.

Meanwhile, Dorothy, her mother and friends waited anxiously for his safe return day by day. However, the time was not far off before they would have to leave.

~ SEVEN ~
Flight from Sissert

British refugees from the Urals

September 1919

The 12 months that followed the assassination of the Tsar and his family had settled into a quiet routine in Sissert. Very little of consequence had happened and people went about their business as best they could. Food was the main problem and many went hungry.

Not unexpectedly, the crisis, when it came took them by surprise. 'The time arrived when the British Consul, Mr Preston, telephoned my father one evening to say that he was making arrangements to evacuate all the nationals in his care, namely Dutch, Italian, Swiss as well as British, and that railway cars would be at the station the next day, ready to leave for the East at noon.' Mistakenly he said 'Bring only what is indispensable, but no valuables.' Dorothy's family should have taken their valuables with them.

The family were up all night packing. By now, they realised it could be a matter of life or death. Little was said; each knew what they proposed to take, everyone with their own thoughts, nerves tense, apprehensive... would they get away in time and would there really be a train for them when they reached Ekaterinburg?

They finished packing early in the morning and left Sissert for good. Their coachman, Feodor, with two Works' horses and Dorothy's riding horse in the shafts, drove them to Ekaterinburg railway station. They said 'Goodbye' to Feodor who left their luggage piled high on the platform as they became part of the anxious crowd waiting for a train.

This happened in early July 1919, when the rooms in the house in Sissert were bright and cheerful, comfortably furnished as usual, the larders and storerooms all stocked up for the winter.

Some months later, Dorothy received a letter from the girl who had given her some lessons in Russian to say that the house had been looted first by the Whites, and again by the Reds on their return. She herself had taken a small Testament from beside Dorothy's bed for a keepsake. Dorothy never heard from her again. Before their departure, Dorothy's father left money for the servants who remained behind, and told them to use whatever was in the house to live on. Dorothy and her father wrote once they had reached Vladivostok but they never again heard from Sissert.

When they arrived in Ekaterinburg, two goods cars were ready for the Italian Nationals. Dorothy had no idea how many there were; the men had been hired from Italy by the builders of a new university to do the sculpture and plaster work on the building, and they were now being repatriated if they wanted to go home. All the heavy boxes and trunks were put into these goods trucks and used as seats or partitions. There was no alternative accommodation for the other waiting passengers for the journey. The train moved off, leaving behind two or three British families, some Dutch people and Dorothy's family's Swiss friends and all those under British protection, on the platform.

An hour later, it was discovered that the stationmaster had been bribed by some wealthy Russian merchant to let him take the railway trucks promised to the British Consul. The merchant had left for the east by an earlier train. The engine for the British contingent was still at the station but there were no carriages. Conveniently, the stationmaster had disappeared, fearing for his life.

Everyone on the station knew that the Reds now had the upper hand in the Civil War and that their army was close by. The Bolsheviks, now in the ascendancy, were slaughtering anyone who had supported the Whites; this would include British and other Europeans who had not managed to escape.

Groups from the British contingent gathered together. They obviously could not go west; abandoning all their possessions and fleeing by horse and cart was a possibility but they would soon be overtaken and murdered. In any event, as far as Dorothy and her parents were concerned, Feodor was by now well on the way back to Sissert.

During these frantic deliberations, an American Red Cross train stopped at Ekaterinburg station on its way to Siberia to combat the typhus epidemic. A Dr Proczech and several assistants were on the platform and offered the bath car of their train to the British contingent for part of the journey. Their bath car consisted of a large zinc-lined bath, the outer side of which was covered with board, leaving a narrow passage between the bath and the side of the car where the men slept. Additionally, wooden boards had been placed across the top of the bath on which women and children could sleep. It was a tight fit, but they all lived there for the first six days of their journey eastward. (The bath would be filled with a solution of disinfectant on reaching its destination so that a number of patients could be immersed at a time.)

At the last minute, before leaving Ekaterinburg two box cars of British soldiers were added to the train. Dorothy seemed to remember that at one time during their journey there were as may as sixty-four cars making up the train.

The train made slow progress, stopping at all the stations however small, to allow troop trains to pass. The distance from Ekaterinburg to Omsk by train is 560 miles. There were three principal stations where they were to stop before reaching Omsk: these were Tyumen, Ishim and Nazyvaemskaya, and there were lots of intermediary stations and unofficial stops in between. At every station, most passengers took the opportunity to buy provisions and to fetch boiling water for tea. During these halts, the British soldiers fetched pails of water or else kicked a football about in the fields. Sometimes, the train would leave without the soldiers, but it went so slowly that the men would catch it by running across the fields to the next bend in the line, when they were always greeted with cheers from those on the train.

It took two weeks to reach Omsk, a very large town, where the British contingent had to vacate the bath car by the next night, with nowhere to go. The American Red Cross train was ordered to go north, where there was an epidemic of typhus, as soon as possible.

Some of the group who were with Dorothy and her family went to call on the British Railway Transport officer for help but all he could suggest was for them to request accommodation at a refugee camp outside the town. This was out of the question; once there, there would still be the problem of getting east which would be made more difficult by the camp's distance from any transportation.

Luckily, the next day a British troop train arrived on the track adjoining the American Red Cross train. Dorothy went out to give sugar to some horses and spoke to some of the soldiers in English when the groom came along to ask what she was doing there. She told him the whole story. It turned out that he was the groom to Col Rodzianko. Col Rodzianko's wife was Irish, like the groom, and interested in the problem of refugees. The groom said he would tell his master all about the plight of Dorothy and her party when he went to report that night and would return as soon as possible if anything could be done to help.

Late that night he knocked on the door, 'It was all right'. The following day, thanks to Col Rodzianko, or rather to his groom, as if by magic a third class railway carriage was produced from one of the sidings. It badly needed repairs so a number of British soldiers came with their tools and patched it up so that the doors and windows could be opened and closed and the bunks secured so that they remained in place without collapsing. Finally, the soldiers scrubbed the carriage clean from top to bottom which was much appreciated by all, as they were to live in this now re-conditioned carriage for the next five to six weeks.

Once they were on the move again, Dorothy gave a sigh of relief. She felt that by now they were far enough away not to be affected by the Civil War and, furthermore, the train was full of British troops who would look after the civilians in the event of trouble.

At some stage in the journey, probably at Kurgan, a goods car was attached to the train taking a number of convicts from a prison in Cheliabinsk, now Celjabinsk, to one in Habarovsk, 400 miles north of Vladivostok; there were also two additional cars of Don Cossacks to guard the prisoners. Now and then these prisoners would try to escape through a hole they made in the floor of the car but they would be caught and flogged. One man was beaten to death. His body was carried away by two Cossacks.

At one of the stops, a flat car was attached to the train, carrying a small cannon on its way to be repaired at an arsenal, with three or four young

Russian soldiers to guard it. One by one these men vanished. The cannon was left behind on its flat car just behind the carriage occupied by Dorothy and the rest of the British contingent. They made good use of it to hang their washing on. The clothes were washed in hand basins which everyone had.

When the British started this journey, the engine driver of the train leaving Ekaterinburg had, for a consideration, been kind enough to let the passengers take hot baths in the locomotive water tender, but later drivers were far less amiable. In fact, the train's progress across Siberia was really in the hands of its passengers. They were often left in open country far from any houses or civilisation of any kind. The driver would de-couple the engine and go off in the locomotive for several hours at a time or even for a day. On his return, he would demand several thousand roubles before proceeding further and if this was not forthcoming, he would go off again, leaving everyone stranded. The passengers would pass around the hat and the driver would carry on for a few hundred miles more before leaving the passengers stranded in yet another field. Dorothy's mother took it upon herself to check the wheels of the British car every day. When a wheel was found to be damaged it was repaired in one of the repair shops in the next station. This usually meant a delay of several days until it was mended. Needless to say it was the British contingent who paid the bill. When possible the 'British' made arrangements for their cars to be attached to whatever train was going east. The convicts and Cossacks had left long ago having been shunted off into a siding at Chita, now Cita, then taken presumably to Habarovsk.

Dorothy and her family were taking the route of the Trans-Siberian Railway. Passing through Barabinsk, they crossed the Chulym River and just before Novosibirsk, the River Ob.

Novosibirsk is the largest city in Siberia. Most of the passengers alighted to buy what little food they could afford and to fill up their bottles with hot water. However, they kept near the train in case it started to move off. The next large town was Krasnoyarsk and on the way they re-crossed the Chulym River. Again, many people obtained refreshments at the station. As the train slowly continued its never-ending journey, the next river crossing was the Enisey River, followed by crossing the Uda River and Oka River before arriving at Irkutsk.

The railway line now skirts the southern end of Lake Baikal and continues until it reaches the town of Ulan-Ude, the capital of the Republic of Buryatia. Here the line divides with the Trans-Mongolian line going south through the Gobi Desert and on to Peking. The Trans-Siberian Railway continues eastward, skirting the northern boundary of Mongolia and continues to Chita, where it divides once more and becomes the Trans-Manchurian line to Harbin and Peking. Meanwhile the Trans-Siberian Railway continues through Khabarovsk on its way to Vladivostok.

Luckily, the train that Dorothy and her family were on now took the more southerly route known today as the Trans-Manchurian Railway, crossing the border at Manzhouli on its way to Harbin. It was fortunate that the train that Dorothy and her parents were on was going to Harbin, as they had friends there who they had lost touch with some time ago.

When the train finally reached Harbin in China about eight weeks later, it was very hot. Cholera was rife and a number of dead bodies lay on the platform waiting to be gathered up. Dorothy's family decided to get a good hot meal at the station restaurant but it was crowded and so full of flies that none of them wanted to eat.

When they returned to their carriage, they were met by a number of English people who had been looking for them for some time. They were members of the British Export Produce company which at that time had agencies all over Manchuria and China. There were two or three men and girls who invited them to their homes for baths and dinner and to enjoy a good rest after the gruelling train journey.

Dorothy thought to herself, 'It was simply marvellous to be in a pretty, cool room, to have a delicious meal at a table set with linen, glass and silver and after a splendid bath, to feel normal for a while and not just refugees. Later, when my family settled in Harbin in 1923, we became good friends with these people.'

~ EIGHT ~
Vladivostok

The wind was pushing me along at a quick run

August 1923

Several members of the British party decided to remain in Harbin and settled there, but the following day, Dorothy and her parents caught another train and continued on to Vladivostok, just over the border into Russia, 300 miles due east of Harbin.

It was now the end of September 1919 or early in October and Dorothy's mother became very ill with a high fever. It may have been sunstroke or typhoid fever. Somehow, Captain John Atkinson of the Canadian Red Cross heard of their arrival: '"British refugees from the Urals, one woman very sick" was the kind of message he would get so he came down the track to see us.'

According to Dorothy 'He was tall, thin, rather bald with the kindest face though rather crumpled. He sent an ambulance to take mother to the American Red Cross Hospital, (the former Russian Naval Hospital). Mother was there for several weeks getting the best of care. My father and I were given rooms temporarily in the British Military Mission's Hotel.'

The rooms were on the third floor, one of which had a balcony and almost as soon as they arrived, Dorothy went out to see what the town looked like: 'Below me was another balcony when a young man with bright red hair came out.' Dorothy knew that a cousin of the family called Alfred Hill was working for British Intelligence 'somewhere in the Far East' and as all the Hills had flaming red hair, 'I called father, who was in

63

the room to come and have a look. "There is a red-haired young man in the room below. It must be Alfred Hill",' I said.

A few moments later he appeared at the door and introduced himself as Alfred Hill. Dorothy and her father saw a great deal of their cousin and his lovely Armenian wife, Marianne. She was quite young and plump, very pale with masses of black hair. She told Dorothy and her father all about her family:

> Some of the stories sounded like fairy tales. Marianne's grandmother had lived in Moscow, so she said, and one Christmas ordered all her kith and kin to come and stay with her for the holiday. She said to the family, 'My first granddaughter to arrive will get a pair of diamond shoe buckles, the second to be born will get a pair of sapphire and diamond buckles, and so on.'

She was fabulously rich; Marianne was the second granddaughter to be born so was given the sapphire and diamond buckles.

Unfortunately, there were hard times ahead when the family's property was confiscated and rich people became poor overnight, eking out an existence by selling what they had managed to put in a purse, their pockets, or to wear unobtrusively. Marianne had worn one buckle made into a brooch the size of a quarter with the small stones in alternate circles of white and blue. She had lovely clothes and had met Alfred when staying in a hotel. Her little dog ran away down the corridor. He caught it for her, they fell in love and married. At that time her English was shaky. They seemed to speak Russian most of the time.

Marianne was popular with all the British Officers. Frequently in the afternoons, a dozen or more could be found having tea with her, especially the young Russian nobleman who joined the British Army and looked very British and handsome in his military uniform. Dorothy remembered Prince Galitzin and Prince Gagarin by name but had forgotten many others.

Dorothy's mother used to laugh at how they made the best of things, at how Dorothy slept on two trunks, the difference in height made up with the clothes they were not using at the time. When Quartermaster-General Robertson, a fat, jolly, red-faced man heard of this he was shocked that they had such poor accommodation and did something about it. A real bed was brought to the house the very next day, after which Dorothy slept on the sofa and her mother on the bed.

When Captain Anderson first came to meet the family in November 1919, he gave Dorothy a job at the Canadian Red Cross. She had never done any office work but he told her she could learn. As she spoke French and Russian she would be the interpreter. Her salary was 500 roubles (rs.500) a month, about ten dollars. Her father got a job at once in the British Army Pay Office, where there were no trained accountants and the accounts were in a terrible muddle. He joined the sergeant's mess and was able to buy cocoa, powdered milk, cheese and jam for the family, as well as soap and candles, these being their staple requirements.

Every afternoon, Dorothy was expected to take a long tram drive from the British Military Missions Hotel where she and her father were living, along the city's main Avenue, the Svetlanskaya, to visit her mother, who was still recovering in the American Red Cross Hospital; she was in a big, light and clean, ward. The nurses were all American and seemed to have a lovely time on their free days. Dorothy never met any of them socially; being a refugee was a stigma. People tended to avoid refugees which was so sad as most were pathetically grateful for kindness. Fortunately, the five or six sergeants in Dorothy's office were always thoughtful and kind to her.

Colonel Douglas Young, who was in charge of the Canadian Red Cross for most of the time Dorothy and her family were in Vladivostok, invited them to a Christmas dinner in his tiny room, where he was living next to the Canadian Red Cross office. 'An Austrian prisoner of War, a handyman at the time, served at table and it was all so like a picnic we could not feel miserable and homeless.'

Dorothy's other friends in the Red Cross Office were two girls, one Mary Cave, the wife of the British Vice Consul, the other a Russian called Vera. The three of them spent the greater part of their time unpacking great boxes of layettes and clothes sent from Canada and distributing them among those they considered the most needy out of the hundreds of women who besieged the office daily; at the same time, the three friends tried to keep lists of the names of the recipients. Russian peasants do not dress babies the way mothers dress them in Europe. Instead, they use swaddling bands and little blankets and the lovely layettes were just sold in the streets to anyone who wanted to buy them.

The Canadian Red Cross Office would often receive long petitions and lists of medical supplies needed by Russian Hospitals and Captain Atkinson and Dorothy would have to drive in an open truck with Nicolai, the driver, to some tiny hospital out in the country. They never seemed to have any patients, just bare, tidy storerooms. Captain Atkinson would give them a few items, but the Canadian Red Cross Hospital had barely enough supplies itself. 'These trips seemed always to be when it was bitterly cold and several degrees below freezing with high winds and as I had no very warm clothes these trips were a torment in winter. I do not remember a single occasion having to go out in fine weather.'

After a time, Dorothy, her father, and her mother, who was now out of hospital, moved out of the hotel to one and a half rooms in a flat owned by Mr and Mrs Verestchagin. Mr Verestchagin was the nephew of the famous painter Vasily Vasilyevich Verestchagin, who came from a noble family and whose paintings can be seen in Moscow, St Petersburg, the Art Institute of Chicago; he exhibited in Paris, London, Berlin, Dresden and Vienna. He specialised in painting war scenes from around the world which he actually witnessed in his travels. 'The Apotheosis of War' depicting a pyramid of skulls, is particularly well known. He died during the Russo-Japanese War when the Russian flagship *Petropavlovsk* was sunk in 1904.

In their new rooms, Dorothy's mother slept on a sofa and Dorothy on their boxes with extra clothes under her to level them up, while her father slept on the sofa in the Verestchagin drawing room. Unfortunately, their hosts entertained a good deal which meant that Dorothy's father was able to retire for the night only after the guests had gone. This flat was situated on Tiger Hill, so-called because the very last Siberian tiger had been killed there years ago. As you go uphill along upper Naberezhnaya passing the Amur Tiger statue, there is a wonderful view of Amur Bay. The whole of this coastline is a series of steep hills. It was on the steep slope of Tiger Hill that Yul Brynner was born at number 15 Aleutskaya in 1920, the grandson of Julius Brynner who built the residence. At the bottom of the hill the sea was on the left, and the main street on the right following the line of the harbour. One day, returning home from town, Dorothy's mother saw several whales spouting water in that bit of sea; she was absolutely thrilled.

'Between 1920 and 1923, life became very dull,' or so Dorothy thought. Dorothy, and sometimes her parents, would go to the Russian YMCA to hear free lectures on raising chickens or whatever it happened to be. There used to be dances at the big American YMCA, a temporary wooden house by the wharf for the US army and navy men. On other evenings, there were dances for the British and French naval men, who got along well because the men from Brittany in France and Cornwall in England were of the same race and spoke the same patois. Sometimes there were boxing matches or wrestling. Now and then the men themselves would hire a hall at one of the schools and have a party with coloured lights, cake, ice cream and cocoa. There were generally two bands, the Marine Band and the Hawaiian Band.

Occasionally, Dorothy and her parents would be invited to a formal dinner or dance by the Captain and officers of one of the US ships. Weekly tea dances at the British Mission were particularly enjoyable and Dorothy made a few friends. There was an occasion on one of the ships when the dinner was nearly over when a marine orderly came and whispered to the Captain who frowned, then said 'I'm sorry, ladies and gentlemen, but the ice cream has just disappeared and we shall have to do without dessert.' The crew probably knew where it had gone.

Dorothy and her parents lived in Vladivostok for the best part of three years. For the first two months, there were riots as the Reds started to push the Whites and foreign troops from the town and there were various changes of government, White cars being driven at breakneck speed along the main streets with shots being fired out of the windows. People ventured out only to work or to buy food, and the next day they heard how many had been killed.

'The twenty-seven revolutions' mentioned by Dorothy probably referred to the unrest that took place between 1920 and 1922. This was the time of the Civil War which was gradually being won by the Bolsheviks, the Reds. In 1920, the atrocities continued; Japanese troops were very active and tried to install a counter-revolutionary government.

By 1922, the Japanese troops were evicted and at the same time the remaining Whites were driven out, amongst them Sergei Prokofiev. Thus, the Reds finally took control of Vladivostok.

In Dorothy's home, bread was their staple food. Russian peasant women baked it in big round loaves and sold it on the edge of the pavement. Every now and then the woman who was most often patronised by Dorothy's mother would ask her to watch the bread while she went on an errand. The usual shops seemed to have disappeared but according to Dorothy, 'Now I come to remember it, the many pawn shops and commission shops thrived, selling furs, carpets, jewellery and silverware. The few valuables people had managed to take with them when they left their homes in Russia, these were eagerly bought very cheaply for dollars by anyone who had the money. The few shops that were open were Japanese, selling lingerie and dresses, also food and fruit shops. Additionally, there was a Chinese photographer and a shoe shop. During these upheavals, most people rented rooms or shared flats. They took their meals in eating houses or small restaurants and sent out their laundry. Dorothy remembers a strange story which came to mind: 'A friend of ours who had the same laundryman for months, always polite in pidgin Russian, and punctual and whom she thoroughly approved, suddenly stopped coming during one of the disturbances. So she hired another laundryman and that was that. Later she and her husband, a Reuters' correspondent, went to a formal reception at which a number of military men of various nationalities were present, British, American, French, Chinese and Czech; to our friend's amazement, a Japanese high ranking officer in a smart uniform with a chest full of medals and orders had also been invited. Many of those present recognised him as their former washer-man. He had been doing secret service work. The story seems to be too good to be true but it was told to us as fact.'

At last Dorothy's father's work in the pay office ended and he and Dorothy commenced working for a Russo-American firm which traded in tyres, machinery and machine tools. The manager's name was Mark M. Atlas; his English did not run to formal business letters so Dorothy translated his from Russian into English, typed and kept the files and earned more than in the Red Cross, about $75.00 a month, which seemed a great deal to her.

Dorothy made a few friends through the Verestchagin sisters, both about her age. As a result, Dorothy was invited to the US Consulate for parties or just to visit the daughters of the Acting Consul, Mr McGowan, and their elder brother, Vassia. Some years later Dorothy met the younger brother, Carrick, in Tientsin, where he was a newspaper correspondent.

The name Vladivostok means 'Ruler of the East' and is the capital of the Primorsky Oblast Province, and stretches up and down a ridge of steep hills along the northern shore of the Golden Horn, extending to Amur Bay. Dorothy was told that, 'Across the bay on another strip of land where the very poor lived, which I never visited, a wretched settlement grew up made of shacks, made of packing cases, tar paper, kerosene tins, Carnation milk cans and mud bricks.'

The hills in Vladivostok are steep enough to have steps for sidewalks; these are of rough stones, cobblestones and wooden planks; on snowy days they were especially bad for walking. On the days when the typhoons blew it was almost impossible to keep one's feet. Dorothy can remember 'The wind pushing me along at a quick run. I would catch a telephone pole and hang on until I caught my breath then let go and run until I grabbed on to the next pole all the way till I got to the office. Unless one's face was covered by a scarf, it would be bleeding from the ice particles the wind flung against it.' A friend of Dorothy was caught in a whirlwind on a crossroad together with a Chinese coolie; they held on to each other while the wind twisted them about then it stopped and they each went their separate way.

In spite of being on the sea, the town became hot and stuffy in summer and one year Dorothy's parents sent her to stay at a summer resort, the Nineteenth Verst, nineteen *versts* from Vladivostok; 1 verst is two-thirds of an English mile and the resort was so called. The beaches were of clean pale yellow sand. The sea is very salty, warm and full of jellyfish, red, green and tiny white ones. The young girls at the resort would go into the water first to pick out the jelly fish which melted when left on the sand, then the little children and their mothers would go in. Dorothy never learnt to swim, but one morning, avoiding a sharp stone, she stood on something flat thinking it was a jellyfish, till it started to move, and she realised it was a crab. She was so frightened she leapt into deep water to try to get away. Fortunately, as the water was so salty and buoyant, she was in no danger of drowning.

Often there would be no electricity in the town at all and kerosene was so hard to obtain that everybody used candles. When there were big parties, hundreds of candles were placed on trays on window sills and on tops of cupboards; it not only looked pretty, but helped to warm the rooms. It was in Vladivostok that Dorothy was first introduced to pork and beans at the home of the US Vice Consul. Mrs Pray came from Boston and at Thanksgiving gave a party at which everyone had baked beans from a big brown pot. 'I thought it was an odd dish for a formal party but I was unused to American cooking and enjoyed being at the Prays.' This was the first family to have invited Dorothy since arriving at Vladivostok. Later, the US Consul General's wife, Mrs Caldwell, used to ask Dorothy, then some of the British residents. Perhaps it was because Dorothy came from Russia was not to her advantage and it took a little time for people to realise that Dorothy and her parents were really British.

In Russia, up in the country, where people are blessedly unsophisticated, no one wore anything for bathing. The country folk considered it 'not very nice' to wear bathing suits so the Russian women bathed in bathing houses. These 'houses' were simply huts built on the river or lake; they had no roof but wooden walls all round and a ledge with a bench to sit on to dress or undress. The hut was probably about twelve feet square and very private, if a bit dark unless the sun was overhead; they had a rather stale smell. The men bathed off the shore at times when people would not be about. 'I remember in Sissert one day in the summer when the weather was nice and hot, lunch was quite late and I happened to look out of the drawing room window and there was our parlour maid swimming in the lake just below, getting cool no doubt, before dressing in her black and white uniform to serve lunch.'

Nowadays, bathing suits are worn by everybody, the Government having become prudish in the USSR.

It was in Dorothy's time the fashion to bathe, take long walks, play tennis and one very old Russian custom where the women went to the station to watch the train come in at five o'clock so as to greet husbands from the office and the summer visitors.

PART II

China
Marriage

~ NINE ~
A Whirlwind Marriage

Give us horses and we shall go at once
November, 1926

Gradually the Russo-American firm for which Dorothy's father was working had to close down, and in the summer of 1923 the family moved back to Harbin in Manchuria for safety's sake. This was due mainly, so Dorothy thought, to the developing political problems in the region; by now, the Bolsheviks were totally in charge having driven out their enemies.

Her father's knowledge of Russian and his experience of business in the East stood him in good stead in Harbin also; latterly, he had been running the British end of a Russian firm which traded in the Far East at that time, in fact, right until the whole of Manchuria was taken over by the Japanese in 1937, when they had to leave.

Dorothy enjoyed her life in Harbin after leaving Vladivostok; most significantly, they had a new status: Dorothy and her parents were no longer considered 'refugees'. They lived firstly with a Russian family in two rooms and then in one of the flats in the Centro Soyas Building.

Dorothy undertook some office work, mostly translating and typing for her father, but parties, tennis and mah-jong took up most of her time. She also took lessons in hat making, taught by a middle-aged Chinese woman. At that time in 1924, cloche hats for women were all the rage and were worn with small brims at the front. Dorothy soon found the amount of shaping and blocking required was relatively easy. Initially, she was taught using linen but later went on to use sisal, a fine straw into which she could weave ribbons. At the time there was a big demand by the 'flappers' in the West for this kind of hat.

Harbin was the birthplace of the Jin and Qing Dynasties and is situated on the southern bank of the Sungari River in the province of Heilungkiang. Originally, it was in Manchuria, until around 1900, when Manchuria was absorbed into China due mainly to Chinese immigration. The railway station was first built in 1899, and is now one of the largest in China. Five railways link the north, south, east and west of the country and Harbin has been nicknamed the 'Moscow of the Orient'.

Harbin is very cold in the winter and hot in the relatively short summer; the temperature varies between minus 16°C to 23°C approximately. It is an important agricultural area and has large areas of forest with many rare animals such as Manchurian tigers, bears, and many species of birds.

In 1926, Dan McLorn, an international banker, a founder member and director of the Hong Kong and Shanghai Bank and a good friend of the family, whom Dorothy had met for the first time at a party in 1923, asked her to take his brother, John, shopping. Dan wanted her to help John buy a number of things he required for his new posting to Urumchi (now Ürümqi) in Chinese Turkestan, in the Chinese Postal Service, where he would be the acting Postal Commissioner for the next three years. Although Dorothy had met Dan McLorn when previously in Harbin, she never considered him more than a pleasant colleague, and she knew even less about his brother John. Apart from family, she could not recall a previous occasion when asked to assist a man with his shopping. However, it was a harmless request and she was happy to oblige.

The shopping was fun; the last item they bought was a long travelling coat of black pony skin, lined in fox fur, with a high stand-up collar of kangaroo fur. John McLorn was over six feet three and the coat reached to well below his knees. To celebrate this purchase and Dorothy's successful bargaining, they had tea in a little tea shop and John, in a businesslike way, asked Dorothy if she would care to go to Sinkiang in Chinese Turkestan with him, leaving in two weeks' time.

Dorothy, taken aback by this suggestion, thought she was being offered a job and refused even to consider it. A little later, Dorothy discovered, by a roundabout way through her father, that this was actually John's idea of a proposal of marriage! Dorothy was now twenty-six, above average height for an Englishwoman of the time, sophisticated when she needed to be, and intelligent enough to assist her father with business matters when he needed help. As a child she had become multilingual and even though she never learnt Chinese at school, she managed to pick it up remarkably quickly in order to speak it in China when most Europeans did not bother.

She had lived through good times in her early life, but knew how to put up with hardship when life was difficult. Dorothy was a level-headed lady, and not the kind of person to get into a flap if things did not go to plan. In character like her father, she was well able to cope in difficult circumstances. She assumed no airs or graces, merely got on with life in a quiet, efficient way, never pushing herself forward, keeping in the background.

As a small girl in St Petersburg, Dorothy had sensed that there was trouble brewing in the city. When the family eventually moved to Apsheronsk, she knew that difficult times were ahead and that subsequent moves only proved her right. At twenty-one Dorothy was most attractive, but now at twenty-six, more mature. It must also be borne in mind that she was in a part of the world where the number of eligible bachelors was limited, and many women of her age back in the west were already married and had children.

John was tall, had a good physique, was reasonably handsome, and was also efficient and intelligent. He had been tutored in Mandarin at Queen's University in Belfast and spoke perfect Chinese. She felt he would respect and look after her. In all probability, John in his turn had surely noticed that here was a pretty, level-headed lady, tall, and reliable enough to be an excellent companion on whom he could rely. His only problem was he was too shy to approach the subject of marriage for fear of being refused, especially as she had already turned him down in rather a brusque manner.

When next they met, she chided him for not being honest from the start. John blushed, trying to apologise, but explained that he was a shy man and did not think she would accept him in such a short space of time. But accept she did.

As John McLorn had been resident in Harbin for only a week, legally, the Consul General could not marry them. To procure a special licence from England would have taken two weeks anyway, so it was decided that he was to stay the extra time in Harbin. A formal request for permission to marry was sent to the Co-Director of Posts in Peking, a Monsieur Destolan, and permission was soon granted. Fortunately, Dorothy had met Monsieur Destolan's cousin at a dinner party, and she vouched for Dorothy being a respectable person. Permission was granted with the understanding that all responsibility for Dorothy's health, safety and welfare was Mr John McLorn's and the Chinese Postal Service would not ever hold itself responsible. All these arrangements took up a great deal of time and tactful correspondence.

After a giddy whirl of pacifying her parents, preparations, packing and parties, they were married on the 21st October, 1926. Firstly, the Consul General, Harold Porter, married them, followed by a short religious ceremony in Dan McLorn's big drawing room, with nearly the whole foreign community present as well as several Chinese Postal officials. Friends had sent baskets of flowers and bouquets as well as boxes of chocolates. After the wedding, Dorothy noticed that these were being 'tidied away' by the servants so they were called back, and Dorothy took the chocolates with her on what was going to be a long journey. The rail journey from Harbin to Manchouli is 595 miles and operated by the Chinese Eastern Express, a branch of the Trans-Siberian Railway.

Dorothy and John started that 21st October 1926 by train to Manchouli (now Manzhouli) on the Russo-Chinese border. John, a sight to behold at over six feet three inches and forty years old, was dressed for overland travel in the ankle-length horsehide coat lined with fox fur which he and Dorothy had bought two weeks earlier. Dorothy travelled in boots and furs. They prepared themselves well with food water, some bottles of wine and warm clothes for their journey.

The journey at this time of the year was the great problem; the snow falls in October and the cold continues for months on end. It would take several weeks and was always difficult. Indeed, it was madness to set off so late in the year, but the Co-Director of Posts in Peking insisted they leave immediately as they had already delayed by getting married.

Manchouli is northwest of Harbin and the train made slow progress,

John and Dorothy
Wedding Photo, October 21st 1926

Family and friends wedding photo
October 21st 1926 in Horbin
Front Row L-R: Dan McLorn, Louise Raitt,
Dorothy and her husband John McLorn, Teddy Raitt

passing through Zhaodong, Anda and on to Ang'angxi, after which a bridge takes the train over the Nen River to Longjiang where the rail track follows the River Yalu.

The train started to climb as the track took a gentle upward incline. Dorothy and John could see the foothills of the Da Hinggan Ling mountain range in the distance as it came slowly into view. By now, the train was struggling and the speed reduced still further. At Zalantun the train stopped.. Apparently, the pass was blocked and it was snowing heavily.

It was now up to the passengers to find their own accommodation. John, who of course spoke perfect Chinese, made enquiries in town and was able to find reasonable rooms until the journey could continue. Although the local Chinese eating houses were numerous, John made sure that he and Dorothy ate at the best.

Eight days passed before news came that the snow had ceased and that the pass should soon be open. Two days later, they were on their way again, but very slowly. They passed through Balin, and Yalu, the town. The train was now progressing very slowly; the lines had been cleared of snow, but ice formed quickly, causing the wheels to slip.

They at last reached Bugt; a few miles further, Xing'an and finally Yilliekede, where the mountains on either side rose to about 6,000 feet above sea level; then they were though the pass to Yakeshi. Here the train stopped and everyone had to leave as one of the driving wheels of the engine needed attention. Once again, Dorothy and John found suitable accommodation until the train could proceed, three days later. At Yakeshi the track turned east on to Hailar, Wangong until at last it reached Manchouli. The journey had taken them thirty-seven days.

In Manchouli, they were the guests of Mr Gibbs of the Chinese Customs Service. He had been English tutor to the late young Grand Duke Alexis of Russia, who had been murdered in Ekaterinburg with the rest of his family. Mr Gibbs had been able to make his way to China and sympathetic people had helped him to this good position. (Dorothy heard years later that he was a thorn in the flesh of the Customs Service.) Mr Gibbs had arranged a small dinner party in honour of the newlyweds. Dorothy mentioned the murder of the Imperial family only because she was '... astonished at these Bolshevik officials' interest in the life of the Imperial family and especially the little boy. Mr Gibbs replied to the many questions but naturally enough did not care to go into many details. It must have made him feel very sad.'

It was now time to say farewell to Mr Gibbs and to continue the next leg of their journey to Irkutsk which is situated on the Angara River some 40 miles south of Lake Baikal and 650 miles west of Manchouli. The town of Irkutsk was developed by the Russians in 1652. Its importance increased very rapidly when the Trans-Siberian railway arrived in 1898 and it became a centre for heavy industry such as engineering, machine tools and mica processing. Most of the surrounding region consists of forests of larch, pine, fir and spruce. The summers are pleasantly warm and the winters exceptionally cold. The border of Mongolia is 80 miles south of Irkutsk.

In Irkutsk, John and Dorothy were obliged to leave their comfortable first class carriage and proceed on 'hard' seats and crowded trains as far as Novosibirsk. On leaving Irkutsk, the train took a north-western direction in a gentle loop, avoiding the Sayan Mountains. Luckily, Dorothy and John had been able secure two seats next to each other. However, they found the journey singularly tedious with the general chatter during daylight hours and passengers moving around at night answering the call of nature.

Some days later they arrived at Krasnojarsk Kansk where the train stopped for a few hours. Here Dorothy and John were able to stretch their legs before returning to the train for a further 370 miles to Novosibirsk. Dorothy remembered Novosibirsk from the time that she and her parents fled from Sissert ten years earlier in 1916. Very little had changed.

At Novosibirsk, Dorothy and John had to part company with the Trans-Siberian Railway and make their way by a local train to Barnaul, 140 miles due south of Novosibirsk and the end of the line. The next stage of their journey would take them to Simipalatinck (now Semeypalatinsk) a further 250 miles. Some years later, the railway line that stopped at Barnaul was extended to the very border of Chinese Turkestan.

It was now up to Dorothy, with her knowledge of Russian, to organise a carriage for the journey. She was fortunate to find a small group of Russian government officials who were also going to Simipalatinck and so they set off the following day, Dorothy and John in a carriage drawn by two horses. On the way, the group stopped at small villages for the night and to rest the horses. John and Dorothy McLorn were now approximately 2,130 miles as the crow flies due west of Harbin and just inside Kazakhstan on the border with Russia.

In Simipalatinck, they were given good rooms in a hotel just across the street from the Chinese Consulate, where John paid a courtesy call which was soon returned by several Chinese Consular Officials. John was now in the Chinese Government Service and not travelling as a British tourist. The Russian Tourist Agency, Sevtorgflot, were reminded daily of their earnest wish to continue their journey but excuses and postponements were all they ever got. The officials did not wish them to travel by horse and covered cart, which they understood was a slow but sure way of travelling, especially in late autumn on bad or muddy roads. The officials insisted they travel by car. The newlyweds were not at all keen on this idea as it meant leaving some of their luggage and two of their Chinese servants behind to follow on later; it was all very unpleasant. One of the hotel guests occupied a room just across the hall and seemed to spend most of his time in their room having glasses of tea, Dorothy and John guessed his job was keeping an eye on them. During the day they used to go for walks about the town where the pavements are of boards about a foot up off the road, inches deep in fine sand; it was hard to imagine how people got about in wet weather unless of course it seldom rained in Simipalatinck.

The log houses were single-storey, the streets neatly laid out; there was a small park with paths and flower beds, a few tired wilted trees and no grass. They visited a cemetery and a church but were cautioned away from a prison by some sentries, so went to the theatre to hear *Aida*, which was very well produced.

As time went by the promised car did not arrive; they waited days and days ... the excuses for the delay were varied and improbable. One car was quite unsuitable, another had to be sent for, then they were told a brand-new car would soon arrive except it had to be first tried out, but it was late ... and so on: 'most unfortunate'. Dorothy had, however, been told to advise her husband that it would be better for his health to agree to travel by car.

At long last the day arrived when they could leave. The car turned out to be a large open car rather more antique than modern, an early 1900's model. There was a driver and his mechanic, some extra cans of fuel and a pail. The car had a leaky radiator and quite often the mechanic would have to borrow a horse and ride off to fetch a pail of water. The journey was slow and they spent several nights in post stations. The post stations were the equivalent of an old-fashioned English coaching inn but desperately dirty and basic; all these stations were poor and wretched. John and Dorothy slept in their clothes in one room and ate the food they had brought for the journey. Boiling water for tea in all these places had to be made available to provide for travellers.

Gradually, the autumn weather changed to cold then to real winter. At this point, Dorothy is vague about when or where they were when the car could no longer tackle the snow and icy roads and had to be abandoned; they were obliged to hire horses and carts but were forced to leave behind many of their warm rugs. The situation worsened still further when one of the horses fell ill and another could not be found to replace it; while the road steadily deteriorated.

At last they reached the border town of Chuguchak (T'ach'eng), within Chinese Turkestan and stayed at a widow's house to wait for transportation across the border. It appeared that there was only one driver with a permit to cross the border with passengers and he was away on a trip. They had to wait. A few days later a Soviet official arrived insisting they had to leave at once:

'Travellers were allowed 24 hours to wait transportation and we had been there much longer'. It was 'not allowed!' Dorothy replied that all they wanted was to leave: 'Give us horses and we shall go at once,' she insisted. He shouted at her and she shouted back, while the hostess paced the floor, trembling with anxiety and crossing herself.

As if by magic, they then heard troika bells and into the yard galloped two troikas with outriders in some kind of uniform, holding big red Chinese visiting cards up in the air at arms' length: 'The Chinese Governor from across the border had sent his soldiers to escort us into Chinese Turkestan.' This was perfectly wonderful from Dorothy's point of view for it gave her husband 'much face' before the Soviet official and better still, was a snub for him.

The Governor Li of Chuguchak was a big, bald man, stout and with a red face. He wore a sort of cowboy hat, baggy trousers and soft boots, the only Chinese Dorothy had ever seen dressed in this way. He understood Russian and even spoke a little. As is the custom, there were no women present when foreign men entered the mansion but they could be heard laughing out of sight in a separate house next to the main building. Dorothy was the only woman present at the formal feasts. He lived in a Chinese-style house, all corridors, courtyards and separate buildings, not at all like the houses Dorothy and her husband were used to seeing. The top halves of the doors and windows were covered with thin paper instead of glass and the rooms were without heating. Dorothy gives a detailed account of a Chinese feast:

The dining tables are usually round, and seat eight. The principal meal begins after people have drunk tea and exchanged formal conversation in another room. One arrives at a Chinese feast 30 minutes or even an hour late. Most of the actual discussions take place over tea before one comes to the dinner table. The meals are elaborate affairs often lasting three hours and sometimes longer. There are many courses but always an even number: 36 or 40. These are carried in also in pairs. Some dishes are exotic, like bird's nest soup or bèche-de-mer, i.e. sea slugs, white or black, or snakes – several kinds cooked together so that the poisonous ones will be counteracted by the antidotes. The most famous dish is perhaps sharks' fins; these do not look appetising in their dried state but when prepared with other ingredients are a great treat and also a very expensive dish. Pork cooked in a variety of ways was also a great standby and in Turkestan one generally had a mutton dish made from fat-tail sheep of the region. If your host gave you a piece of the fat-tail, you ate it with apparent pleasure as this was a great honour – the same applies to the eye of the sheep. The host uses his own chopsticks to proffer this delicacy. The use of chopsticks is at first difficult but with practice they become easy to manipulate. It is not considered good Chinese manners to eat much and I have heard that guests often come to a feast after the usual meal at home and only taste and nibble after much persuasion on the host's part. Warm rice wine is poured from a very small teapot-like containers into tiny wine cups.

Dorothy always thought rice wine smelled sour and warm which put her off, so never tried to taste, and never did, drink it. Brandy is also served at big parties. A little rice wine goes a long way and the men often leave a party a little worse for wear; this is not considered bad form, rather the contrary, the host feeling that it is a compliment that his guests enjoyed themselves so much. Dorothy often used ask for a glass of tea to drink during dinner and found it easy to fill the little brandy glass with spoonfuls of tea. 'I hoped that no one noticed and I do not think they did for I had a reputation for drinking a lot and not showing it! A rice dish is the last to be served so that people will know that it is the end of the feast and time to leave with elaborate compliments on both sides and deep bows with one's hands clasped at one's waist.'

While in Chuguchak, Dorothy and John stayed at the Post Master's house. The Governor must have moved his family out of the best room, where they were very comfortable, if bored, in spite of their usual walks and some new acquaintances they made among the local Russian community; here again they had to wait.

While waiting for Chinese immigration officials, dressed in military style uniforms of green, to permit them to continue on their journey to Urumchi (now Urumqi), they spent time walking around each town where they were detained. Here in Chuguchak, the snow was already deep and John had no winter footwear. They searched in all the little shops but no boots were large enough.

One day, when walking through the market, they saw a tall Khirgiz nomad (Khirgiz is a Chinese ethnic minority who come from the prefecture of Xinjiang), walking about. They stopped him and through sign language and the help of an interpreter asked if he would sell his truly huge felt boots, *valenki*, from off his feet for a good price. *Valenki* are Russian boots made of wool felt which at first were worn with galoshes to keep the soles dry, but these had vulcanised rubber soles. The nomad was extremely doubtful, but with a bit more encouragement and persuasion, he took them off and John quickly put them on before he had time to change his mind. Dorothy wondered how the nomad managed to get home.

Some three years later, when Dorothy was travelling through this same frontier town, her luggage was turned upside down over the counter at the Customs. Her Tartar travelling maid was not allowed to continue with Dorothy and was turned back, but the Customs official remembered Dorothy from several years ago, especially as her husband had on his feet the biggest pair of *valenki* he had ever seen. Dorothy didn't like the official any better the second time they met as he was the same man who she had rowed with when told that travellers were allowed 24 hours for transport across the border and that she and her husband had been there much longer.

Because of the weather conditions, John and Dorothy had overstayed their welcome in Simipalatinck, but now in Chuguchak the snow was falling heavily and the chances of proceeding on to Urumchi was unrealistic. At least they were in Chinese Turkestan and couldn't be blamed for the weather. John was becoming increasingly restless, conscious of the fact that their departure from Harbin had been delayed due to his marriage to Dorothy. He did not want to let down Mr Destolan the Co-Director of Post in Peking, who had given him permission to marry and it was up to him to get to Urumchi by any means possible. But how?

~ TEN ~
The Silk Route

The Oriental merchant is a patient man

Mid-November, 1926

It is possible that John and Dorothy knew they were on the border of Tarim Basin, the world's largest, dominated by the Taklimakan Desert, Urumchi (Wulumuchi) to the north, Hami to the east, Charchan (Ch'iehmo) to the south and Kashgar (K'oshih) to the west. The Silk Route also passes through this desert though the route Dorothy and her husband followed was a little further north than that taken by Marco Polo. Marco Polo was a Venetian traveller and businessman born in 1254 and, in 1271, at the age of seventeen, he was one of the first Europeans to travel overland to China. He met and soon became a favourite of Kublai Khan by whom he was employed for 17 years. The route between Venice and Changa'an (now Xian) in China, became known as the Silk Route, which extends over 5,000 miles. Early travellers from China brought silk, spices, lacquer ware and clothing, but particularly silk for which there was a great demand, from the east, for sale in the west,. There was no single route between the two cities but each depended upon oases where travellers could stop for refreshments and supplies.

The two main routes ran north and south of the Taklimakan Desert. The northern route, starting from Xian, goes through Lanzhou, Turfan (Turpan, an oasis), Hami (now Kumul), Urumchi (Urümqi), Kuqa, an oasis, following the Tianshan mountains in the north of the Taklimakan desert and on to Kashgar (Kashi) where it joined the southern route.

Dorothy and John were to join a section of the northern route on their way to Urumchi. The temperature in the desert varies enormously depending on whether it is winter or summer. In about 1400, at the end of the Mongol Empire, the use of the Silk Road ceased, mainly due to the development of European maritime advances, which made sea travel cheaper quicker as a means of trade between East and West.

Dorothy writes:

The snow had been falling steadily for weeks – the roads blocked for miles. Rumour said that a big caravan of goods that local merchants would be transporting was leaving as soon as the weather had settled and it had stopped snowing ... The caravan would 'break the road', i.e. pack the snow and we could follow their trail; that sounded so good that we postponed our departure from day to day.

The caravan was to go from Chuguchak(Tacheng) to Turfan, the next oasis past Urumchi, on the Silk Route:

'The Oriental merchant is a patient man; the caravan did not start, he was waiting for us to start so that he could follow ... At last a message came from Urumchi begging the new Postal Commissioner (John) to hurry up ... By now, the snow on the road was up to the horses' shoulders.'

The generous Governor of Chuguchak lent them his smart sleigh and team of black horses and a driver for the first day's stage, which brought them about 40 miles to Omin (now Emin). After that they had to continue with hired teams, travelling at a snail's pace:

'The horses would take five struggling steps and would have to stop to breathe and rest, then five more heart-breaking steps and rest again.'

In this way, Dorothy and John reached the next post house at Mopan (now Toli) before dark and stay till morning light, then continue for another day.

'These post houses were small, dark mud huts with a *kang* on one side.' A *kang* is a Chinese stove for warming rooms and can also be a brick or wooden erection for sleeping upon, warmed by a fire placed beneath. Blankets were laid on top to sleep on and sit on to eat. Dorothy and John ate the same thing every evening: boiled meat of some kind or whatever they could buy, sometimes a duck or pheasant cooked over a small fire.

Camel or cattle dung was used for fuel; wood or coal are unknown in this region as it is desert country but then of course, they always had tea. Sometimes they could buy the local bread, flat unleavened thin loaves, baked on the outside of the outdoor ovens with the family's boots drying out beside it, as well as other garments.

'The cold was intense, my husband became feverish and ill. A painful and infected throat prevented him from speaking or eating. The canvas of his camp bed tore almost every night so as soon as we made camp, I got out my thick needle and strong thread and sewed the canvas together, it never held up longer than a night and was a great nuisance. Still this mending helped to pass the time till I went to sleep.'

They progressed on: to Maio'ergou, Uzunbulak, Xinchepaizi, Wusu (now Usu), Shihezi, Manassu (now Manas), and finally Urumchi, a distance of 280 miles from Chuguchak.

On one of their many halts during their progress, John had a bad sore throat. It happened that the old gentleman at whose house they spent that night was a doctor of Chinese medicine: 'He suggested a cure, merely a herbal brew, he could prepare but only if the patient would promise faithfully to drink it. By that time, the patient would agree to anything as his fever was worse and he could not eat and we had to continue the journey. So the brew was made and when brought it looked like pale coffee with leaves and sticks standing up in it; I felt that there were beetles and things in it too but did not enquire. Anyway, my husband drank it down and rushed immediately out to the yard where he was violently sick; he came in paler than ever and a bit shaky but the fever subsided, the sore throat was better. He was cured.'

Before they left the next day, Mr Li, a Chinese Postal clerk on his way as Russian linguist to the Post Office in Urumchi, and travelling with them, came and asked Dorothy to intercede for him to her husband. He wanted to marry the young daughter of the house and take her along with them if he were permitted: 'I was astounded and it was only much later that I understood that Mr Li had probably arranged to stay at this house for this reason. The girl was a regular country bumpkin, plump, rosy and silent and dressed like a peasant in red trousers and a blue jacket with her hair in a thick plait down her back and the fringe over her forehead that all girls wear until they are married.'

Room was found for her and her few possessions in Mr Li's carriage and so she joined the party.

There was no letup of the freezing cold and high winds, and the post houses on the journey left a lot to be desired. A week after leaving Chuguchak, John and Dorothy were invited to pass the night in a *yurta*; this huge felt tent belonged to a prosperous Tartar traveller. As far as Dorothy could remember there was probably no rest house in the vicinity: 'The *yurta* was a big tent twenty feet in diameter, full of boxes and hung with rugs and it seemed to be full of people but we were made welcome. However, my husband was afraid of lice and bed bugs so our camp beds were made up in the shed that was next door to the tent, but where it was so cold that I never closed my eyes.'

Dorothy rather envied a pretty woman fellow traveller who slept in the warmth of the tent, and when Dorothy mentioned vermin the woman said 'Well, what of it, one may as well scratch, there is nothing else to do on a long journey.'

Some of these desert stages were merely for rest and a night's shelter for travellers and their horses and camels, but were so miserable that there was not even a spring where one could get fresh water and what water there was tasted brackish, so the next stage would be a short one to a spring of good water.

The caravan which left Chuguchak after John and Dorothy had now almost caught them up. They were now crossing a level plain called La Fung K'o, the Mouth of the Wind, in the afternoon, when a hurricane blew up. There was a clear blue sky, and later, when dark, with stars visible right above their heads, the whirling snow nevertheless hid everything around them. The drivers could not see their way; the horses just stood with their backs to the wind, heads down. Dorothy and John simply sat in their sleigh and kept alive in the extreme cold by drinking wine they had with them in the luggage. By six in the evening they had all lost their sense of direction and had no idea where they were. The Uigurs of Chinese Turkestan believe this desert to be an evil place where people can go mad and as a result many strange legends are commonplace.

The drivers all gathered together in one of the carts and kept their spirits up by singing. The snow flying about was so thick that Dorothy was sure that they were deep in the forest, which gave her a feeling of being stifled. At two o'clock in the morning, their group was found by a mounted military search party sent from Wusu, the small town they were making for, by the Post Master of the place, who was expecting them and feared for their safety.

A flat sleigh was brought and Dorothy was helped on to it, she was quite helpless both from cold and blindness; she held her arms in front of her to avoid hitting herself against the imaginary trees as they moved off.

Three years later when driving across this plain on a lovely day in May, Dorothy saw it as it is: flat, bare, and empty save for occasional stone walls built to shelter shepherds and their herds in storms. There is not a single tree anywhere in the Mouth of the Wind.

In Wusu, they were given a fine clean bed in a warm room in the Post Master's house and rested well, but they were lucky. The servant's son, a boy of fifteen, Len Chi by name, had wanted to go for help in the night with another man. Len Chi could not ride and was thrown off the horse. He fell in the snow and just lay there until found by one of the search party, alive, but with his hands half frozen. Before Dorothy went to bed to rest she implored him to keep out of the warmth and try to keep his hands in cold water till they revived. On awaking, they found Len Chi, in a bad way, sitting by the stove in their room. The time had come for John and Dorothy to continue the journey but had to leave behind the poor boy, who was too ill to travel. Nothing could be done to save his fingers. Much later, the postal doctor in Urumchi amputated the black remains of most of Len Chi's fingers. He had a thumb and part of a forefinger left so he was able to get an education in Chinese and be taught Russian and ultimately Dorothy believed he got a job in the Postal Service as a Russian linguist. Originally, he had been hired as cook to John.

They lost sight of both Len Chi and his father; the latter was a man typical of the ideal Chinese family servant of the old regime; his manners were excellent, a good manager, cook and general factotum, he never complained though he must have been very lonely. A man from Peking thinks only his own city is civilised and the Chinese who live in Turkestan are quite different from those in the homeland; he could have no friends.

By now, Dorothy and John had covered around 3,500 miles since they started their journey westward:

'We had left Harbin in China on October 21st and had been travelling by fits and starts until December 24th by which time there were but a few miles to travel before reaching Urumchi. It was a fine very cold bright day, a road snow-packed with damp snow drifts on either side. Suddenly we were met by a most elegant traveller, a gentleman, in a handsome sleigh pulled by a pair of frisky greys and driven by a Tartar coachman.'

The gentleman got out and of course, Dorothy and John had also stopped. He approached and introduced himself as Constantine Cymrkin, and offered to drive Dorothy quickly into the city as their horses were tired and slow. Dorothy thought she must be tired so got into the sleigh and when comfortably settled under the fur rug, off they went at a gallop: 'The driver was obviously very competent and wanted to show off the horses'.

Away they sped, when suddenly the sleigh swerved and Dorothy flew right into a snow bank. It was really funny but the coachman lost face for tipping Dorothy out of the sleigh. It appeared that this coachman turned out another passenger on a previous occasion and felt that he had lost so much face that he moved out of Urumchi to the heavily faulted Altai mountains, east of Urumchi.

Mr Cymrkin owned ranches and gold mines in Russia and was involved in shady political transactions. He was of Cossack stock and an astute business man. Sad to say, he came to a miserable end; all his wealth was of no avail. He had sent his wife and three children to the United States and he himself died unhappily in a Chinese prison. He was greatly disliked for his shady dealings and his riches. Dorothy felt very sorry when she learned of his fate, as she found him jolly and most pleasant and she liked his whole family.

Chinese Turkestan has long been a place of exile from China, perhaps as Australia in the early nineteenth century was from Britain. It is a vast, rich country, fertile, beautiful and interesting too. Marco Polo travelled through this region along the Silk Route from India to China in the thirteenth century. During Dorothy's life and since, travellers have rediscovered the Silk Route and have written books about it. The authors Dr Sven Hedin and Owen Lattimore, with his wife, often visited Dorothy and her husband in their house while living and writing in Urumchi. This is a country that has suffered war for centuries and until the 1920s, there were wars between the Chinese and the Mohammedans. It is common when travelling between the various districts to see great mounds of earth some only ten or fifteen feet high.

If you question the origin of these mounds the reply is always predictable. A Chinese person will say that Mohammedans sacked and burned a Chinese village years ago, whereas a Tartar or Chanto would say that the Chinese burned the Tartar villages. The races do not like each other; there is envy and scorn and distrust, although when necessary they do business together and seem friendly enough. Many Chinese are of the Mohammedans faith and it is possible to guess which they are by their names: Har, Mah or Ma were the ones that Dorothy was familiar with and knew.

The women in wealthy Tartar families are strictly secluded in Urumchi and seldom left the women's quarters and if they did it would only be at the New Year to visit female relatives. They were muffled up to their eyes and travelled in a closely curtained conveyance accompanied by young men, relatives, on horseback, brothers or cousins riding alongside the cart. On one occasion, Dorothy's doctor's wife took her to call on a friend of hers, one of these Tartar women. The friend was born in Russian Turkestan and spoke the Tartar language perfectly. She was greatly respected for her education and wisdom because she sometimes interpreted for her husband, Dr Podeshenko, when he was called to Mohammedan houses. He spoke French and German well but not the local tongues. Dorothy found the conversation among the women rather dull as far as she was concerned but the hostesses were interested in Dorothy herself, as they had never seen a foreign woman before and were full of questions and compliments.

The man of the house was a rich merchant whose name, Tursan Baba, sounds as though it came from the Arabian Nights. These people distrusted paper currency and banks and kept their wealth in gold coins and gold and silver ingots, called 'shoes' in China, from their shape, that of a Chinese lady's shoe.

The house, which Dorothy visited, was Spartan: a table at which all the women had tea, a few straight-backed chairs, and some heavy looking chests against the whitewashed walls. There were no children to be seen but they may have been kept out of the way. Boys live in the women's quarters until they reach the age of seven; then they live with the men and only come to visit their mother and sisters occasionally. The boys go to school to learn the three Rs but, in the 1920s, not the girls, although this situation has almost certainly changed within the last forty years.

There is sure to have been a mosque in Urumchi, but Dorothy could not remember seeing one nor hearing the muezzin calling the faithful to prayer three times a day, as she did when visiting a little place called Manass.

Dorothy and John used to drive with a team of horses to Manass to shoot geese in the spring and autumn. But it was John who did the shooting while Dorothy stood with a spare gun beside him in twelve inches of chilly water among reeds with an eager pointer beside her. It was nearly dark when the sky would turn pale grey and the noise of millions of geese would come nearer. It was easy to shoot as many as John wanted; he couldn't really miss. As for the ducks that also took to the wing, well they weren't worth a shot. Jimmy, the pointer, carefully carried the dead birds out of the deep water if that was where the game fell and laid the bird always at John's feet. The first afternoon they arrived at Manass the sky was so dark that Dorothy thought it was due to snow clouds but soon realised from the noise that the whole sky was black with geese.

It was now the end of December, 1926. John and Dorothy were about to start their married life in Urumchi, a strange place of many interests and hardships, where many women from the west would never dream of visiting, let alone going to for a honeymoon.

~ ELEVEN ~
Life in Urumchi

A Chinese servant does one job only

Summer 1927

After the desert and inhospitable landscape that Dorothy and John had been travelling through they finally arrived at Urumchi; on 24th December, 1926. The name in Mongolian means 'Fine Pasture' and to their great relief it they found that it was surrounded by oases in an otherwise vast plain of grasslands and largely treeless terrain. The population of Urumchi was predominantly Chinese but includes many minorities such as Khazak, Uighur, Manchu and Tungkan peoples.

Urumchi, also known as Urumqi, or Wulumuchi or Tihwa, is the capital of Chinese Turkestan, a province bigger than France and Germany combined. The town is situated near to the north face of the T'ien Shan mountains, about 8,000 feet above sea level, while the summer camps in the foothills of the T'ien Shan mountains are some 2,000 feet higher.

South of Urumchi, about a day's ride away, is Turfan, only 250 feet above sea level in the extraordinary Tarim Depression and therefore it has a much milder climate. Here the people grew grapes in huge quantities, also peaches and apricots, all of which were halved and dried in the sun on tables covered with nets to keep off some of the flies. These are sold with an almond on each half. A handful of these dried apricots make a satisfying snack. From Turfan also come the celebrated Turfan melons; so special are they that camel caravans of melons used to be sent to the Emperor in Peking every year, carefully packed to preserve them on the long journey.

In Urumchi, there grew a fruit new to Dorothy: 'It looked like a Chinese crunchy pear which is rounder than our pears (in the west) and green, but it had a peach stone instead of seeds. This could have been a nectarine.'

A Chinese acquaintance, Mr Ah, not an official, had an orchard and Dorothy and John had been to some tea parties to view the blossoms or the fruit in season. Chinese town gardens are very different from a typical English garden: no lawn, no flower beds, some flowering shrubs in tubs or vases; urns with peonies, oleanders, chrysanthemums and sometimes a large container with water for ornamental fish and always a high wall all round for privacy.

The day after John and Dorothy arrived at the Postal Commissioner's Residence in Urumchi it was still occupied by their predecessor, Mr Cavaliero, and it was Christmas Day. The Postal doctor and his son George arrived about eleven o' clock to pay a formal call. Other than English, John only spoke Chinese; the Russian doctor spoke German and French and Mr Cavaliero spoke French ... They all began as they continued throughout their stay in the Province of Sinkiang, with at least three languages being spoken at once. Of her first day in Urumchi, Dorothy writes:

'Later that day three troikas full of young people came, this was the choir from the Orthodox Church to bid us welcome in songs and carols, a lovely thing to have thought of and which I never forgot. The choir was excellent, the concerts and plays arranged by that small Russian community were well produced and usually performed in someone's emptied living room with kerosene lamps or candles for lighting. The music was played on guitars and balalaikas, old tunes people could dance or sing to.'

Dorothy and her husband brought Fox Trots into fashion and the One-Step (which became the Quick-Step in America. In England it was better known as the Castle Walk and as a Fox-Trot variation). Dorothy showed the men how to do them while John danced with the girls. One girl who was too tall and rather plain was nicknamed 'camel' because she was so big and no one bothered to ask her to dance till John, who was even taller, singled her out and she became very happy and a good dancing partner. The young men never let her sit out after that. She soon married one 'and lived happily ever after'.

Looking back on these people, Russian émigrés of all classes, Dorothy found it odd how few of them she ever got to know intimately, over the period of two years and five months when she finally left Urumchi. There were the two doctors, the Cmyrkins, the Jewish manager of the Russo-Asiatic Bank, a German businessman and his delightful wife, her sister and her husband; the sister was a very pretty, flighty woman whose affairs were an unfailing topic of gossip. There were also the two Roman Catholic priests and of course, the four British China Inland Mission representatives. In Urumchi Messrs Hunter, French, Ridley, Mather and Mann, and three ladies of that mission, were always travelling far inland, while Dorothy stayed in Turkestan. She only met them some years later in Tientsin. Miss French and a Miss Mildred Cable, another member of the British China Inland Mission, wrote several books on their journeys around Turkestan.

It is true to say that one must eat and drink one's way into Turkestan and then drink one's way out again. Everyone welcomes and entertains the new arrivals and speeds parting friends. You meet scores of strangers and eat innumerable delicious meals all endless and so friendly in atmosphere that strangers could not feel like strangers for long. Then when the time comes to part it all happens again. People with horses accompany the departing ones for at least half a day's stage, when yet another meal is eaten, a picnic this time, healths are drunk and one is off.

When they first arrived in Urumchi, Dorothy and John stayed for a time with the Roman Catholic priest, Father Hilbrenner, S.J. He was a huge, genial, red bearded man nicknamed Father Barbarossa by his many friends. He spoke good English which was a boon to John who knew little French, no German or Russian and had to speak Chinese to their Russian and German friends in Urumchi. There were two schoolmasters, some merchants and some men who were in minor positions in the Chinese government service. They were all émigrés. There was a Soviet consul general and his staff who did not mix with the rest of the non-Soviet members of the Russian community. When Dorothy arranged a party at home she had to be careful which guests to mix. On the more formal occasions she invariably invited one of the minor Chinese government officials; knowing that all that occurred in the house would be reported to the Governor. It was more sensible to have a guest report than a servant, who could make trouble by inaccurate reporting.

It was at one of these dinner parties given by John and Dorothy for a number of postal clerks over a year later, when next they met Mr Li and his 'country bumpkin girl', now his wife, who had joined them on their journey to Urumchi. They were among the guests:

'She now wore her hair coiled on her neck, no fringe, a silk gown, earrings in her ears and rings on her fingers. She was as plump as before but looked prosperous and happy.'

Probably Mr Li had a wife at home in China but she would be too precious to be made to travel in hardship and discomfort, so like many other Chinese, he got himself a 'travelling wife'. The Chinese are practical in other ways too: if a man and his wife have no children, especially no son, it is the custom to adopt a nephew who is then brought up as their own son. One of Dorothy's servants did just that, and adopted their nephew Kung Pao; the servant's wife bore three children some time later.

In the summer of 1927, when the Governor General himself honoured Dorothy and her husband by accepting an invitation to dinner, it was all 'really hectic and funny in some ways'. Governor Yang had bought a big Packard car from Dorothy and John's predecessor and was driven the short distance from his palace to their house. His military escort, some forty strong, in bedecked uniforms were mounted on sturdy ponies and rode in front of and behind the car. The roads were full of holes and high stopping posts (where pedestrian are allowed to cross the road) ready for the summer season, so the cavalcade, though impressive, was slow. The other officials used Peking carts (a Peking cart is a horse drawn carriage) or rode horseback, some also with a military escort. As a result, the yard was full of ponies and Peking carts and the front hall full of soldiers. The bedroom doors were locked and knick-knacks put away in other rooms. The soldiers were given cigarettes and money and as soon as the dinner was over and the dining room empty, they charged in and finished all the wine left in the glasses. Happily, there was never any trouble with these people.

Almost always, Dorothy was the only woman at formal Chinese feasts. Chinese wives, especially the young women, were considered too precious to be displayed in public. These feasts were held roughly at three-monthly intervals in different houses. The wife of the Governor General, Yang, and the wife of the Foreign Minister, Madame Liu, were sometimes present; they were, Dorothy remembered, rather pretty, well preserved, dignified ladies with shiny black hair and smooth skins, dressed in dark satins and damask silks stiff enough to stand alone; their shoes, too, were of black satin. In those days, Dorothy could not carry on much of a conversation as her knowledge of Chinese was almost nonexistent; John or one of the Chinese clerks had to act as her interpreter.

'At home, one of the servants, Kao Ti by name, was the coolie who did all the odd jobs about the place, a good man though not bright by any means; he was so old fashioned that he wore a queue (pigtail) down his back while the rest of his head was shaved. He was the only Chinese I have ever seen with a queue. This man did my shopping in the local shops for me – you see, a lady never went beyond her own courtyard unaccompanied so unless I drove in the carriage with the coachman or rode or walked with my husband, I did not go out into the city.'

Kao Ti would buy thread or cotton print for Dorothy to sew; she made appliquéd curtains and bedspreads for the bedrooms and table cloths for the dining room. 'My instructions were in sign language plus samples of colour and he never made a mistake.' He hardly ever wore anything on his head. Dr Pedashenko said 'his brains had been frozen' because his head always shook slightly.

In addition to Kao Ti and the number one boy who had been with John for years, they had a cook, two house coolies, and a gateman, whose only duty was to open and close the main gates; Dorothy never saw him doing anything else.

Whilst in Turkestan, Dorothy and John were sometimes reminded of scenes that could have come from the Bible. On one occasion, they saw a man in a long robe wearing a turban kneeling on a prayer mat on a hillside and praying at sunset. At the foot of the hill stood his young servant holding the pony and the ass.

In the countryside away from Urumchi, they frequently watched local tribesmen out hunting with great, tall, hooded hawks on their wrists and their hunting dogs, the rare Saluki breed, running beside the pony:

'The clothes worn by these men were like those in cowboy pictures, soft leather boots with high heels, baggy sheepskin trousers or leather ones with fringes, high fur caps with long ear flaps and sheepskin coats. They seemed to wear the fur inside for warmth in cold weather, and outside to keep off the sun's rays in summer.'

The house in which Dorothy and her husband lived in Urumchi was of red brick and one storey. It had an open verandah through which one came to a large square hall from which opened the dining room on one side and the pantry beyond it. The drawing room was on the other side of the hall and there was a long corridor straight ahead. Three bedrooms opened off the corridor, the end one being the guest room followed by a primitive washroom beyond it. The master bedroom had an opening off the washroom and was claimed to be the only bathroom serving three bedrooms in the whole of Chinese Turkestan:

'True, the water was stored in a large tank above the tub to which a coolie carried pails of water up a ladder when it needed filling. Hot water for a bath was likewise carried in pails from the kitchen.'

Dorothy's house was furnished by the government to exactly the same standard as all the other postal residences in China. It was easy to recognise the dining room and drawing room suites because even the slipcovers were the same in most houses; only the carpets and draperies were different. In Urumchi, the beautiful Indian carpets had been woven to order so that they fitted each room perfectly. The carpets looked new in spite of having been down for years. The surface had been swept clean with brooms, but never had a broom been deployed under any furniture. When reorganising the furniture after Mr Cavaliere left on home leave, Dorothy was horrified to find dust three inches thick beneath every chair and sofa. The only pictures on the walls were posed photographs of postal employees and of travellers with camels and carts and tents which Dorothy took down and replaced with reproductions of paintings cut out of art magazines.

Mr Cavaliere had however, left behind one great improvement: a really good wine and store cellar. It was reached by means of a trapdoor which was kept locked, and could only be entered by way of a ladder kept in the study. The temperature in the cellar was ideal for the wines. John used to get wine from Shanghai and many other stores in Peking. Unfortunately, the wine took over a year to arrive always via Peking and by camel caravan so Dorothy and many other people living in Urumchi had recourse to making their own. Dorothy would order ten donkey-loads of grapes which made 400 bottles of wine. No sugar or water was ever added. It kept well, though it was seldom kept for long in most houses; in

Dorothy's cellar it usually kept for some months. The servants helped to press the grapes by hand, and with a hand press; when the wine was ready, all the servants – even the gateman – were given a bottle. The juice made pale or dark-yellow wine, the pressed skins produced rosy to dark red wines: 'I only mention this as some people may be interested in the hobbies of people who live in the wilds of Chinese Turkestan.

'A Chinese servant does one job only. A cook cooks and does the marketing. One coolie does housework, and the other kitchen jobs. With no central heating, electricity or plumbing there is much more to be done by hand. These people had a kitchen and quarters of their own at the back of the house where I never went.'

A servant usually dressed in baggy trousers of blue or black cotton, padded in winter, and in the house, wore black soft shoes, white socks and a scrupulously clean white coat; when serving at table, he wore a long white coat. Every Chinese has one good long silk coat in a dark colour for New Year or for important occasions, and a round black skull cap to wear outside the house. The women servants dress the same, the only concession to fashion (which the Europeans never noticed) may be the width of the sleeves or the length of the jacket or the length of the slit at the side.

Dorothy and her husband's bungalow in Urumchi was just inside the East gate of the city; this was also the main gate which, along with the other gates in the North, South, and West, were all very heavy and made of wood about 15 feet apart. They were always locked at sunset, the key being handed to the Governor himself every night. Apart from the East gate, the other gates were less important and caravans both camel and horse and huge carts would enter and leave the city by these gates.

The whole city was surrounded by a stone wall about forty feet high and more than eighteen feet wide at the top. A two storey gate-house stood over each door and was inhabited by a garrison. Each morning at sunrise, the great gates would be opened with an iron key some eight inches long and closed for the night at sunset, which in winter would be shortly after three in the afternoon. This meant that if Dorothy and John invited guests who lived in the Russian factory outside the walls, where most of the Russians lived, they had to leave the party soon after dinner. Dorothy used to feel quite embarrassed as she never got used to the gateman coming to the drawing room door and reminding the guests to please start going home as the city gates would soon close.

The city had about 20,000 inhabitants who lived in houses built of mud bricks. The streets were usually wide; there were no sidewalks or pavements but there were rows of stopping posts standing here and there to enable people to cross the street during the muddy season, at which time the mud was thick and inescapable and vile smelling, embellished by puddles as big and deep as ponds, in which donkeys and small children had been known to drown. As soon as the mud solidifies enough to be worked, it is mixed with chopped straw, then poured into moulds for bricks and dried in the sun. After which, the bricks were used to repair houses in need of patching or to build new ones. The sun gradually dried the mud in the streets, when they became deep in dust until the winter.

Dorothy records her observations of the camel caravans:

We liked to watch the camel caravans; they pace slowly. In the spring their heavy wool coats moult and come off in patches so they look moth-eaten. The camel-puller walks in front of the camel or alongside it, and pulls off the wool and spins it into thread as he walks. Now and then a mother camel carries her newborn baby in a big flat basket tied to her back. The baby cries for its mother and she calls to it, thinking it is lost. If a baby is soon due, the mother walks with the basket empty on her back. The camels lie down to be loaded with heavy packs on either side of the hump. They grumble and scream when they have to rise – this is an uncomfortable and awkward kind of scramble. Camels and horses hate each other and never seem to share the same inn yard. While we lived in Urumchi, many of our supplies came from China by camel caravan and many stores were lost when some poor camel fell down a precipice. Camels do not feed by night as horses do so the caravan rests a day here or there on a journey so that they may feed on the grass by the way.

Just outside the East gate was a little house where the city's beggars lived. Any horse or cattle that died was usually dumped at the beggar's house; the carcass did for many free meals. Begging was not a disgraceful profession in China, not like that of a soldier, who in those times was despised. A beggar was a person who had his pitch and made a living asking for alms. Each locality has a King of the Beggars who gets a percentage of the take and settles disputes.

'In Tientsin in the 1930s, John was passing a German cake shop on his way to the UNRR office very early one morning when he saw a well kept car drive up and the crippled beggar who always sat at the shop door got out. So he obviously made money begging. He and my husband were used to greeting each other to the embarrassment of one of our children. In Harbin, a hunchback beggar always stood by the tennis club and my mother used to give a quarter to him every week and he never begged from her at any other time. Beggars' children are taught to beg, especially the crippled, deformed or ones with epilepsy.'

In Sinkiang, any able-bodied beggar, or even a criminal, would be drafted into the army and sent to a faraway district.

Criminals were generally severely punished; the commonest crimes seemed to be robbery and banditry. Once on his way to the Post Office, John's carriage was stopped by a soldier who said 'Just wait a minute.' This happened near the market square. A prisoner, his hands tied with string, was taken from a cart in which he had been driven about the city, receiving small presents from sympathizers. He knelt down and the executioner cut off his head. The carriage transporting John then continued on its way to the office.

In the summer of 1927, Dorothy joined her friend Madame Pedashenko and her young son, for a summer holiday of over two months in the mountains. They took three *yurtas* with them as well as bedding, pots and pans and other household items. Dorothy also took a folding chair, two camp beds, a folding table, a little stove and even a window. Like all *yurtas,* it was a round tent made of heavy, camel-wool felt strips, securely fastened by cords onto a trellis of wood about four feet high. Long canes are fastened to this, all pointing up to the centre hoop, so that the tent is some seven or eight feet high in the middle: 'The native women can put one up in a few minutes, a man never does this job.' Dorothy made the *yurta* most comfortable, and was so sorry that John could not spend his three short weeks' vacation with them but he could not stand the seven or eight thousand foot altitude; it made him feel sick and too giddy to stand upright. He soon went back to town.

There was little they could do to amuse themselves except to ride or walk in the forest and look for berries and mushrooms, of which there were many edible varieties. One of the Roman Catholic priests stayed in their spare tent as a guest and a number of other friends joined them a little later. Dorothy and Madame Pedashenko hired a Khirgiz couple to look after them: a little boy to fetch wood and water, and an old man to be a shepherd. They bought mutton on the hoof and at one time had a little herd of nine sheep. They bought cows', sheep or goats' milk from another camp and this interchange meant that all these people and their relatives were their protectors and took care of their interests, so they would never be robbed or offended by strangers. The *yurta*'s door was merely a flap of felt tied in a bow to the next piece of felt. When tied it was considered locked and no local would try to enter.

These Khirgiz are a nomadic race and wander all over the mountains with their herds of horses, goats, sheep and cattle, moving to new pastures from one valley to the next with their tents and household goods on the backs of oxen. Their womenfolk also ride on the horses. The men ride if necessary and can ride very well. The ponies are very sure-footed and Dorothy had seen them gallop, then slide all four feet together down a steep mountainside, being ridden by a woman, a baby in her arms and a bigger one hanging on to her belt behind. The Khirgiz are olive-skinned, dark-haired, and often have rosy cheeks and always bandy legs from a lifetime in the saddle. The women wear a piece of white cloth around their head and face: 'I was told this was their shroud which was worn till they died and were buried.'

The slopes of the Tien Shan range are wooded on the north side and grassy on the southern slopes; edelweiss (the star-shaped, white, velvety flower of the Alps) grows ten inches tall, with gentians about six inches. In the Swiss mountains they are less than half that height. Pretty streams abounded, and Dorothy could make camp anywhere she chose. Some of Dorothy's Russian friends had a summer camp several miles away. She and Madame Pedashenko visited them one Sunday and enjoyed an Orthodox church service in the forest: 'The religious icons were hung on the trees and a wooden plank on two tree stumps was the altar.' They started back home soon after tea as it gets dark early in the woods. When meeting natives out riding in the mountains everyone stops for a chat. 'They always ask who you are, where you've come from and where you're going.'

Young Pedashenko always maintained that Dorothy was his sister. Once a week, John sent Kao Ti up to Dorothy with provisions, including rice, cabbage, bread, salt and sugar and cake and fudge packed in saddlebags on their old horse, Staryk, so they were well cared for. Dorothy's friend, Madame Pedashenko, had travelled to the mountains in a carriage; George, her son, rode a pony and their luggage and three *yurtas* were packed onto one of the great carts with six-feet high wheels to go over the bad roads and to ford the streams. The great carts were pulled by a team of horses or oxen. Dorothy travelled on a cart like this when leaving Urumchi. It is like a covered wagon; the blue coolie cloth kept out the sun and the occasional rain.

There are only about ten days of rain in a year but miles and miles of irrigation ditches make up for this. The water flows down from the mountains as the snow melts and the farmers use it as they need by damming up streams and opening the sluices when their fields need irrigating. There are two or three crops a year. The winters are very cold for about four months. Before the last snow melts, grass shows up on the sunny side of the hills and just outside the east city gate there were thousands of irises in all shades of yellow and purple.

Mr George Hunter of the CIM had been asked by a horticultural society in England to send them various types of iris roots, but he refused even to think of it, although he spent all his life and energies travelling about Singkiang trying fruitlessly to convert the Mohammedans. He was a saintly old gentleman, one of the greatest collectors of Moslem books and manuscripts of which he had a valuable library. It was suggested to him that the Bodleian Library of Oxford was the safest place to hold this priceless collection, but he insisted that it be kept in an indigenous little house occupied by three missionaries in the city of Urumchi, 'For the young men who will follow me,' he said. For obscure reasons, Mr Hunter was arrested and thrown into prison, where he died at last at eighty, a martyr to his faith and Scots obstinacy. The last time that Dorothy and John saw Mr Hunter was in Shanghai, where he had to go on business; he did not care for Shanghai at all, saying that he much preferred the desert and the lonely places of Turkestan. He knew the common Moslem language of the country as well as Chinese and had prepared a dictionary and grammar book. All his work and his fine library were lost, unless they've been kept by the Russian linguists.

The official language used in all China is Kuanhwa. This varies with the district; as a rule, though it can be understood, the differences are very noticeable between the north, south, east and west, even between places as close as Peking and Chefoo. The locals understood them better than the Europeans did but never laughed at their foreign pronunciation. There are many dialects which are as different as French is from English. It is not uncommon for discussions among Chinese from different districts to use English. Dorothy heard pidgin English being used in her kitchen if, for instance, she had borrowed a servant for a dinner party who was not a northerner as all her own servants were. Their two *amahs*, maids, were from Shanghai and Dorothy used pidgin English to speak to them. Dorothy knew people who had lived in China for twenty or thirty years and had never bothered to learn or to speak Chinese. Among Dorothy's associates, pidgin, in either French, English or Russian, was a nice and easy way for busy or lazy people to converse. Dorothy could speak Chinese in a shop, hire a rickshaw or greet a friend of one of the *amahs*, but could not manage an hour of polite small talk with a Chinese woman acquaintance; fortunately their husbands knew at least one European language and could translate.

There were to be further language problems just a few months after Dorothy and Madame Padashenko had returned to Urumchi but of a most interesting and amusing kind; the difficulties involved the use of many different languages all at the same time...

~ TWELVE ~
The Sino Swedish Expedition

Miss Nina de Torgut of Peking
January 1928

In early 1928, Sven Anders Hedin, a well known Swedish explorer and author, at the age of sixty-three led a Chino-Swedish scientific expedition to Mongolia, Western Kansu and Sinkiang. He came to Sinkiang to rediscover the Great Silk Route and some interesting geographical peculiarities of the land around Tarim River, which flows into Lop Nor Lake 280 miles southeast of Urumchi. He had with him a number of scientists who were specialists in their fields, as well as an artist, a doctor and linguists in Chinese and Chanto. Most of these scientists were young. There were Swedes, Danes, Norwegians, Chinese and Germans. Dr Sven Hedin himself spoke many languages and the others several each.

Toward the end of February, Dr Hedin and his colleagues arrived in Urumchi where they were invited to dine with John and Dorothy at their house. The conversation was very amusing as half a dozen languages would be used and there was much laughter and great appreciation of the reception they received. The Governor, General Yang, did not care to open his frontiers to foreigners at the best of times because of the difficulties of the situation where the province of Sinkiang was surrounded by the Soviet Union, India and Mongolia. Fortunately, Dr Hedin had made his request for permission to travel for scientific purposes through Dorothy's husband, John, a friend of Governor Yang who had been able to arrange permission with his opposite numbers in the surrounding countries.

During their stay in Sinkiang, the Expedition made detailed maps of

Taklamakan desert and the ancient Silk Road. While he was in Urumchi, Dorothy took Dr Hedin and a few of his colleagues to see, in the local museum, the mummy of a woman believed to have lived between 2000–1800 BC; the mummy had been discovered in the Taklamakan desert. The unusual thing about the mummy was that she had auburn coloured hair and was thought to be of Caucasian origin; what then was she doing in this part of the world?

The Expedition had rented some buildings in a Russian settlement outside the walls of Urumchi which served as base camp while some of their colleagues were out in the wilds gathering scientific data. The Expedition remained there for about five months and during this time Dorothy and John were invited to some great Scandinavian feasts. These parties, which were held in the camp, lasted until well after midnight so they were invited to sleep at the house of Dr Padashenko, where he lived with his wife, his son and his partner. Dorothy and her husband would arrive at the doctor's house at around 3 p.m. before the city gates closed. It was still possible to enter the town through a wicket gate:

'After one of the parties we, the two doctors, Ambolt from the Expedition and Padashenko and his wife, their young son and another lady, also one of the young men of the Expedition, started for the Padashenko home at about two in the morning hoping to escape meeting the Watch on their rounds; one was not supposed to be in the streets late at night. (When anyone went out after dark they had to carry a large lighted lantern with their name in Chinese characters in red paint eight inches high on the side.) Unfortunately, we did meet them: half a dozen soldiers or police who asked who we were and so on. My husband spoke Chinese fluently and offered to be the spokesman but our young friend was overexcited and waxed angry and rude in Mongolian to the Watch. A soldier struck him and he was arrested and led away. When my husband tried to interfere he was hit over the head with a rifle butt, his face was cut, luckily his high collar of fur protected his head. We took the lady friend home and then made our way to the Padashenko house where we were all given a dose of bromide, a large bottle of which was always kept on a table in the living room in case of need. It was a nervous life there.'

A note was quickly written to inform the Expedition about what had happened to their member, but since the streets were not safe to use at this time of night, it was a problem to know how to contact the Expedition. As is common in many Asiatic cities, the houses are built close together, the doors and windows face the inner courtyard, the street walls are blank and the roofs flat. The note therefore was given to a small boy who worked as a helper in the kitchen. He was awakened and told to go and hurry to deliver the note to the Expedition and no one must see him. So away he ran across the roofs of the houses at three o'clock of a bitter winter's morning and delivered the note. The members of the Expedition rescued the prisoner in the morning, sober and very apologetic. John received a formal apology from the officer in charge of the Watch in question.

Another well known Mongolian Dorothy and her husband entertained at this time was Kalmyk Princess Nirjidma Torgutska Palta, born in 1907, the daughter of Prince Palta (1882–1920), who was the administrative ruler of Sinkiang:

'The Princess was educated in Peking and in France where she made her home. She was small and pretty, vivacious and attractive to men, her clothes were beautiful. She was otherwise known as Miss Nina de Torgut of Peking, Paris the Sorbonne and other places – typical of those coming for no particular reason, she arrived in January 1928 and at once became a welcome addition to parties given by the Sino-Swedish Expedition and later by the Citroen outfit'.

Nina remained a good friend of Dorothy and John until they had to leave but she stayed in Urumchi for ten years, returning to Shanghai in 1938 with her husband, a Kalmyk nobleman, where she gave birth to two sons. After the death of her husband, the colourful Nina married a French Consul, Michael ———, the aristocratic manager of Havas News Agency headquarters in Shanghai:

'Eventually, having got on the wrong side of the Governor, allegedly having schemed against her own brother a Mongolian princeling of ancient and noble tradition: the Khan of Kara Ossun, she and her husband returned to Paris in 1950. She spoke Chinese, French and English besides her native Mongolian and seemed more French than Oriental. She died in 1983.

'For several weeks over the years we entertained at our house Lt Col

R.C.F. Schomberg, D.S.O., a delightful person who was in the British Government Service. He had retired from the Highland Regiment he commanded and now travelled about with several Pathan servants and a small caravan. He wrote rather dull scientific books and articles for the Royal Central Asian Society, [established in 1901 and now known as the Royal Society for Asian Affairs], and the Royal Geographical Society, both of which my husband was a Fellow. While Col Schomberg lived at our house, two of his servants used to wait at table or walk behind me if I ever ventured out on foot alone.'

Dorothy was expecting her first child in November 1927 and after the first three months of pregnancy she felt very well. Early summer is the best season of the year in Turkestan, so she and John went to visit friends in the Russian Factory, a settlement much the same as a Hudson's Bay Trading post. They also went for long walks in the country along the banks of the Urumchi River which flows through the centre of town from East to West. On the east side, the 'Red Hill' slopes steeply upwards amidst densely packed pine and cypress trees. The hill is roughly a mile long, half a mile wide and rises 1,700 feet above sea level; its name comes from its reddish-brown rocks. In 1785, the river overflowed which gave rise to many superstitions at the time.

On one occasion, John and Dorothy took a high wheeled cart to a valley 47 miles to the south of Urumchi to a river of spectacular beauty. While walking along the river bank they saw a number of pheasants and a colourful 'Ram Chakor'. The valley ended where a waterfall of 130 feet cascaded down a precipice hidden amongst trees, spraying upwards a rainbow of fine droplets of water as it struck the rocks.

Official dinners were fairly frequent all the year round, mainly with high-ranking Chinese officials such as Governor General Yang, the Minister of Education; Liu Ting Zang, the Minister for Foreign Affairs; Fan'Ta Jen and members of the Consulate General of the USSR.

After one of these formal dinners in May, she and her husband were asked to dance 'the Modern Way' to entertain the other guests. At that time Dorothy was in no state to show off, as she was heavy with child, and refused. Her hosts were not prepared to accept her refusal until at last John unfortunately lost his temper and struck one of the guests. There was a tremendous row. Telegrams were sent to Peking to the Department Head and even to the President demanding the recall of John McLorn.

By the time Dorothy came to writing about this incident, which had upset her greatly, her memory became clouded as her mind was fully occupied with other things like the preparations that needed to be made for the birth of her child.

With the onset of winter, snow covers all the ugliness of the surroundings and the city looks clean for an hour. There is plenty of traffic. The big carts, drawn by mules or horses or sometimes by donkeys, but donkeys usually carried loads in panniers – kindling wood, coal, straw or hay, even tubs of water from a 'good spring':

'I remember one winter we thought it would be delightful to enjoy the city snowbound and lit by moonlight – all very black and white and quiet, just the sound of our passing in the sleigh. We did this for several nights but then it seemed these trips were unorthodox.'

The trips displeased some official and they had to end this simple pleasure.

The streets were not lit up at night. Peking carts had tiny candlelit lanterns on one side of the front end of the cart. Pedestrians however, carried big paper lanterns 17 inches by 12 inches, some red with the owner's name in black characters, others white with the name in red. When opened and carried, the shape was a rounded oval. They were carried at the end of a stick. No one ever went out after dark without his lantern which had a candle.

Electricity was still rather a novelty in the 1920s. The Chinese officials had it in their houses and the government offices, but it was unreliable so that John's predecessor preferred to keep to the old kerosene lamps which were always to be trusted. Telephones were unheard of in Dorothy's time. She said that they wrote notes instead and the coolie took them and waited for an answer.

Dorothy writes:

We bought a pretty donkey, whose job it was to fetch drinking water (in two tubs hung on either side) from a good spring three or four miles away on a hillside. This spring formed a good big pool some 12 feet across and many women used to come here to wash their clothes. Others used to wash their clothes at the warm springs in the country to the east where there were many hot springs. One used to see Mandarin ducks which are orange in colour swimming there during the winter. Then there were always stately camel caravans. The camels tied nose to tail wore specially shaped bells on their necks. Peking carts on high wheels harnessed to ponies and all the riding public, Khirgiz, Mongols, Chantos and some Europeans of whom there could not have been more than a hundred or two at any time. I may mention the fact that in our time in Urumchi the nearest British Consul was at Kashgar, near the Indian and U.S.S.R. border and was a forty days' ride on horseback away from us, 40 days for letters and one more for people. The Russian community was sharply divided into the émigré families who had fled the 1917 Russian Revolution and who had been well treated by the Chinese Governor General, and the members and sympathizers of the U.S.S.R. who kept very much to themselves. There were those who also had a foot in either camp. We used to call them the 'pinks' – neither White Imperial loyalist nor Red Revolutionaries. Several of the Whites had taken Chinese nationality. All these Russians lived in the settlement to the west of the Chinese beyond the wall. It was called the Factory like the Hudson's Bay factories of long ago or settlements where the 'factor' traded with the natives for furs and skins. It is interesting to note that the British colony one hundred years ago in St Petersburg was headed by a group called, "The Factory." I vaguely remember my mother telling me how proud they were when my father, while still quite young, was elected a member of 'The Factory' in St Petersburg.

The houses in the Russian factory in Urumchi seemed to consist of just one long street of houses, whitewashed and quite plain, some were hidden behind walls and stood in a big yard which contained the shed for the animals, the kitchen, the servants' quarters and sometimes another two or three roomed little house – always single storied with 'the convenience' tucked away in the barn. The official and Government officials' houses were of grey or red brick. Some of the better shops were also of brick and grey in colour. Shops seemed to have wide-opened double doors, a few steps up off the road. They were very dark inside, much of their display of wares was hung on strings along the ceilings or on the open door. Nearly all the merchandise came from Russia, some from 'the coast' as China was called. Several of the more wealthy Chanto merchants lived in the Factory. There the Russo-Asiatic Bank had its office and the manager's flat in the same building. Mr Mark Feldman was friends with both the Red and with the White Russians. He was the only Jew there that spoke English well. He was the host on numerous occasions when we had to come for an evening party in the Factory, having had to leave before the gates closed at 3 p.m. It was at Mr Feldman's flat that I first tasted instant George Washington coffee.

When Dorothy and John first arrived in Urumchi in December 1926, short skirts were being worn everywhere, but not in Urumchi. Here ladies still wore dresses about ten inches off the floor; being plump was not considered ugly, chignons were usual but lipsticks were admissible though silk stockings unobtainable except through friends in Peking or Shanghai. As there were no shoe shops, it was probable that footwear was being made locally by a cobbler or sent from China. Men wore top boots most of the time which looked all right as their suits tended to resemble a uniform. Their manners were as polished as one could hope for, with even a little more hand kissing than was necessary. On the other hand the USSR officials were less demonstrative to say the least. Dorothy's powers of translating from Russian to English and back again were severely taxed – especially when jokes and anecdotes followed the dinner. By the time an English joke had been turned into Russian, it was never amusing.

Dorothy writes that 'Russian women did little housework themselves. Young Moslem or Chinese boys were glad to earn a little money and to get enough to eat by working for the Russian families. The lady of the house cooked for special dinner parties with the servants helping her. Mutton, beef and all kinds of fowl were served, never pork as the Moslems may not eat it on religious grounds. Chinese cabbage, garlic and onion, carrots and potatoes were obtainable. The Roman Catholic priests grew more exotic vegetables such as cauliflower and broccoli. We grew tomatoes cabbage and some other green stuff – until I became ill, even willow seeds were sown by me and had some years later grown into fine large trees, I heard to local surprise, as nothing was supposed to grow in our compound. All it needed was water and people to use it. A stream flowed just below our outer wall until the dry season, after the snow had finished melting up in the mountains. Rain was unusual but heavy when it did come, not more than ten days in a year.'

On one occasion John was asked by Governor Yang to interpret at a secret meeting with a government representative of another country. It was a very important and secret affair and Dorothy writes:

'The Governor said he could trust no one of his own staff... My husband agreed to do this but I knew nothing except that the talks had gone off satisfactorily.'

Later, John became Liquidator of the Russo-Asiatic Bank. Governor Yang was a tall old gentleman who looked exactly like one expects a Chinese Governor General of a great province to look like: calm, dignified and silent. He was pale and wore a small white beard. He was a just ruler and a stern one, but good to his trusted friends.

'Governor Yang had one son, a mischievous boy of about eight who, when he came to one's house and admired anything in the room he expected to receive it as a gift and generally the host did present the article to the child be it a camera, a dish of sweets or some other coveted thing.'

Dorothy made a habit of hiding anything of value before any of her guests were expected.

Dorothy was by now becoming rather tired and her back was painful. She was of course nearing the time of her confinement and everything was a great effort. Dorothy had the disposition of someone who could always cope whatever life threw at her. However, she could never have expected what was to happen within the next couple of months.

~ THIRTEEN ~
Life and Death, 1928 – 1929

I was still in a state of shock

On the 28th June, 1928, Dorothy was delivered of a son by the light of a kerosene lamp and two candles. The postal doctor, Dr Pedashenko, saw to the birth, helped by a Russian woman who was called in. It was a natural birth: no anaesthetics were used, as there were none, then or later, in order to apply stitches to close a rupture.

Every item of medical supplies had to come from Sinkiang, Shanghai or Peking; the orders took anywhere from six months to a year to arrive. Supplies came by parcel post, that is by camel caravan, when roads were impassable for wheeled carts with wooden wheels six feet high.

'Normally these carts,' Dorothy tells us, 'were used for transporting goods, though I have travelled in one with a blue canvas top, like the covered wagons of the American settlers.' All means of transport were slow. It was necessary therefore to send medical supplies in solid or powdered form which were 'made up' locally. The doctors were adept at using local items and skills. Thus an exact diagram of the surgical instrument he required had to be drawn by the doctor. Later on the parts of an electrical massage machine had to be made for treating Dorothy's paralysed face and limbs. These artefacts were produced by the local Chinese blacksmith and a Chanto watch repairer.

In the first week of July, early in the afternoon, Dorothy and John were disturbed by the sound of shooting. This seemed to come from the city below and to the west of the postal residence and went on for several days and nights. Dorothy was weak enough to be still in bed after the birth of her son but begged to be told why everyone looked so sad and anxious. She was not reassured by what they told her: 'When I was told that the Governor General and many others had been murdered it was a great shock to me.'

The leader or instigator of the revolt was the suave Mr Fan, the Commissioner for Foreign Affairs. He was very friendly with, and influenced by, the Soviet-Russian Consulate Staff, including a youthful and attractive typist and stenographer named Zoya, an excellent Chinese linguist. Fan Ta Jen must have intended becoming the next Governor of the Province and so the old General Yang and his eighteen years of peaceful and paternal rule was swept away at one stroke with the Russians supporting Fan himself.

Governor Yang was killed at the annual banquet of the Urumchi Law School after several days of fighting in the Yamen, the official headquarters of the Government. This banquet was attended by most of the officials of the government and some Russian teachers. The Governor was always accompanied by his personal bodyguard, a stout Chinese in a black uniform and a moustache. He stood behind the Governor General's chair. At some moment during the feast, Mr Fan excused himself on the pretence of a matter of business, whereupon his guards fired at the Governor. His bodyguard threw himself before his master and held him in his arms but it was too late. Governor Yang had been shot through the back.

Mr Fan hurried to the Yamen to quickly take possession of the precious seals of office. But he was trapped by a fellow conspirator, a Mr Chin, who also meant to become Governor. In the presence of the old Governor's troops, Chin accused Fan of the murders and ordered his arrest, displaying the invaluable seals of office as proof of his authority. The infuriated soldiers shot down and killed Fan's military guard of a few score men, whereupon Fan himself was put in a pillory. He was exposed to public view in the Yamen courtyard for a day, spat upon or beaten by anyone passing by. Needless to say, he was condemned to death, but first the soldiers slowly tortured him, then cut off his limbs and finally his head.

Chin took office as Governor of Sinkiang after an 'official election' so to speak. A few years later, Chin narrowly escaped a similar fate by travelling to China proper: 'I remembered he lunched at our house in Tientsin, a heavy-looking rather silent person, definitely in need of funds. I never heard what happened to him.'

Neither Dorothy nor John ever wanted to see Chin again and never did. Some of the details given above on the assassination of Governor Yang and subsequent developments are borrowed from an article on Sinkiang written years later by two friends of Dorothy who lived in China.

Mr Fan's little daughter (he was a widower) was saved by her nurse before she could be murdered by the furious crowd and was somehow spirited away to safety.

After these riots, other people who had tried to flee were caught and killed. The radio man ran across the rooftops to escape but was hemmed in by the soldiers and killed. The shooting went on for three days and nights near to where Dorothy and John lived and many of their friends were among the officials who died.

What with the delivery of her baby, which was not easy, and hearing of the assassination of old Governor Yang, whom Dorothy liked and respected, she became very ill, with either a cerebral haemorrhage or spinal meningitis; she never discovered the exact nature of the illness:

> I was unconscious for many days and paralysed down the left side. Dr Padashenko moved into the guest room and lived in our house for three weeks, being determined to pull me through although it was a pretty hopeless case. Dr Hedin's medical adviser, a Dr Ambolt who travelled with him said, 'Why prolong the poor woman's suffering? She can't see out of one eye, she is paralysed and she is in great pain.'

The old Russian priest in the Russian Factory Church, after Morning Prayer one Sunday, announced a 'Service of Intercession' would begin for the return to health of Dorothea Feodorovna (Dorothy's Russian name). The whole congregation remained to take part. 'I was unconscious for days with the pain in my head,' Dorothy says.

The doctor wrote in his report: 'The invalid, though very patient, screams in pain'. Five ice packs surrounded her head with a hot water bottle at her feet to draw the blood from the head. Leeches were unobtainable to draw the blood off the brain. At last the doctor tried making tiny punctures behind each ear and drawing out the blood with a breast pump:

'At first,' Dorothy writes, 'the blood was very thick, but after some days the operation being repeated night and morning, the blood became the usual bright red, and the pain, I should say, was relieved from the very first day of bleeding.'

At the end of July, 1928, Dorothy and John bade farewell to Sven Hedin and his Expedition. A week had hardly passed when the 9th Panchen Lama, Tubdain Qoigyi Nyima, the Mongolian living Buddha, passed through Urumchi and visited Dorothy's house.

The Panchen Lama is the second highest ranking lama after the Dalai Lama. All Buddhists consider him a reincarnation of Buddha and in their eyes he is a God. Nyima was very well dressed, short and thickly set with the rather highly coloured face of many Mongolians. 'He was dressed in dark-blue mufti, a Nehru coat and seemed a quiet, shy young man,' Dorothy observed.

This was the time in history between 1913 and 1950 when, to all intents and purposes, Tibet was an independent nation though nominally under Chinese suzerainty.

The baby thrived:

We had bought a little cow so that he could have the same milk all the time… It was feared that even when I was well enough to be carried out on to the verandah and then began to walk again that I might drop the child out of my one able arm, so that I was never able to play with him nor hold him myself. He was a bonny, rosy fair-haired child.

In May 1929, Dorothy left Turkestan for good to go to Lausanne in Switzerland to try to recover from the long illness she had suffered as a result of the shock of Governor Yang's assassination. Her baby and a Tartar nurse were to have left for Lausanne where Dorothy hoped that intensive physiotherapy would cure her left side. Unfortunately, her lovely baby became ill two days before they were due to leave and on May 13th, 1929 he died of spinal meningitis, aged nearly eleven months: 'My Russian friends sent a few home-grown pink roses to put on his plain wooden coffin. Everything that had been in the nursery was burnt, clothes, bedding and all. It was decided that I had better leave as had been originally planned and this I did.'

Permits had to be obtained and travel arrangements made months earlier for the child, Dorothy and the Tartar nurse to travel with one of the Danish members of the Sven Hedin Expedition, who was returning to Stockholm through Russia. Henning Haslund Christiansen had an important mission to perform for Dr Hedin:

'The latter had procured a Mongolian tent completely and exactly furnished as a travelling Buddhist temple.' This he was presenting to the King of Sweden and Haslund had the job of taking it to the King:

The tent was erected in our courtyard and a Mongol came to arrange it correctly so that we knew what it would be like in the Stockholm museum. The prayer wheels, their holy book, coloured pictures, many little silk flags, hangings and tassels looked a bit tawdry and shabby to the eyes, but as it had travelled far – that would be perfectly natural. All of this was to be presented to the King of Sweden by Haslund from members of the Expedition and especially from Dr Hedin. But unfortunately, the Swedish newspapers which reported all this very fully, rather tended to 'write up' Mr Haslund, who was tall, blond, blue-eyed and charm personified, instead of his leader, Dr Sven Hedin, the famous explorer.

Dorothy was still helpless, not being used to looking after herself with one hand: 'My hair was no trouble since it had been shaved off completely the year before and was still very short.'

When they reached the Soviet frontier, the Tartar maid, Mariam, had to return to Urumchi as she was not permitted to proceed further, so Dorothy was forced to cope all alone: 'Selfishly, I had left my husband on or about May 16th, 1929, travelling with a Tartar woman in a big cart, Mr Haslund in another and the luggage in yet another. I wore riding breeches and midi blouses were comfortable for climbing onto the high wheeled cart and even in the train later on in the journey.'

Fortunately, Dorothy spoke Russian fluently and some Chinese but Mr Haslund spoke only his native language. However, he could carry the bags and cut up Dorothy's food, so that they were able to help each other out:

'When Mr Husland and I arrived in Semipalatinsk, a large town in Russian Turkestan, we tried all the inns and hotels where my husband and I had waited so long, three years ago, for the Sevtorgflot travel agency to get us transportation – but nowhere could rooms be found. It was quite possible that no hotel was permitted to accommodate foreigners. At last I remembered I was the wife of a Chinese Government Official and we drove to the Chinese Consulate General. I hoped to impress the local inhabitants and addressed myself in very shaky Chinese to the amiable people who came out to speak to me. All our problems were soon solved. We were invited into the office to have tea and never has tea tasted so refreshing.'

Several of the Consul staff occupied rooms in the hotel across the road. These were given to Mr Haslund and Dorothy, the Chinese moving into the Consulate office. During their stay at the hotel they were entertained by the Chinese Consul. All were as kind and helpful as one could wish. Dorothy and Mr Haslund left by train three days later.

Dorothy does not record the details of the rest of the trip from Semipalatinsk (now Semey) to Helsinki in Finland. However, she and Mr Haslund must have travelled back along the same route that Dorothy had taken many years earlier through Omsk, Ekaterinburg, Moscow, and St Petersburg before finally arriving at their destination.

Here in Helsinki in Finland, Dorothy had several relatives, some Finnish, whom she did not know, apart from her adored and devoted aunt, Miss Nika Raitt. Nika had received a telegram telling her that Dorothy would need a nurse to travel with her to Switzerland. Nika Raitt had not heard of the death of Dorothy's son and had interviewed several women willing to travel, the most promising was to come to meet Dorothy. Unknown to Nika this lady was also a qualified masseur whom Dorothy hired at once, despite not having a child, but as a masseur. Fru Thyra Sjoblom had dark hair, blue eyes and was a trained Swedish masseuse.

Dorothy now had to go to Stockholm with Mr Haslund, where she was invited to stay with the three Misses Hedin before proceeding to Switzerland. The Misses Hedin lived in one of the fine houses right on the quayside in Stockholm, in a huge apartment, furnished in handsome antiques of dark wood and bronze inlay. There were masses of books everywhere. All the Swedish and foreign editions of Dr Hedin's books were together on the great bookcase. The three Hedin ladies all spoke English fluently and were most charming, especially Miss Alma, who arranged money matters, tickets and so on. But, Dorothy writes: 'I was still in a state of shock and different from my usual normal self.'

Mr Haslund and his brother-in-law had a big party at the Stockholm Tivoli Summer Gardens on Midsummer's Eve when it was still daylight at eleven at night. Everyone talked, ate and probably drank too much and joked the night away.

Mr Haslund's brother-in-law had a delightful summer retreat and invited Dorothy to stay for a few days. Miss Hedin said she would have to come as a chaperone, which made the men roar with laughter! Dorothy would be the chaperone they said, being the married woman while she was a spinster. Miss Hedin looked a well-preserved fifty but could have been fifteen years older. Her brother always looked fifty even when quite elderly.

Dorothy and her future companion and masseuse really got to know each other on their way from Stockholm, where she joined Dorothy, to Lausanne. She spoke Swedish, but Dorothy did not. However Fru Thyra was born in Russia and still remembered a little of the language. At the beginning, it was rather a struggle, but they got on famously.

Alas, in Berlin, while waiting for the train, Dorothy had a convulsion, frothing at the mouth, jerking her limbs and finally becoming unconscious.

This was not uncommon after Dorothy's illness and happened quite often, sometimes several times in one day, induced by excitement, worry or any strong emotion:

'I took some pills for this ailment, naturally, and outgrew it in about thirty years. My companion was frightened but stayed with me and was very good, calm and sensible. She was very religious, a thoroughly good person with one grown-up son, a schoolboy son and a young daughter. She had been widowed many years earlier.'

Dorothy decided the name Fru Thyra Sjoblom was a bit of a mouthful 'so I began calling her Abigail for short'.

Because of the bad fit Dorothy suffered at the station in Berlin, she could not remember the details of the journey to Lausanne. The fit was almost certainly epilepsy due to the cerebral haemorrhage or spinal meningitis she had suffered in July, 1928.

Although by now it was getting late in the day. Abigail was able to reserve a couchette on a wagon-lit for Lausanne. The journey of about 580 miles as the crow flies took around fifteen hours with a change at Zürich.

It was now early in July, 1929. Dorothy's aunt, Alice McCallum, had reserved a large double room in the Hôtel des Étrangérs for her and Abigail, who was to stay with and to look after Dorothy until John was able to get three months' home leave.

At the time of Dorothy's arrival to sojourn with Aunt Alice, she had an acquaintance staying with her while his wife was in hospital having a baby. The father-to-be introduced himself to Dorothy and Abigail. There was old Madame Renévier and her elderly daughter. They were frequently visited on a Sunday by her son of whom she was very proud: 'Mon fils, le Général,' in the French Army; he was a stout, ruddy-faced man.

There was also Dorothy's great friend, Miss Hebe G.P. Hunter, with whom Dorothy had corresponded for many years until she died in England in the fifties, an aristocratic Englishwoman of the old school. Her cousin had represented the Viscounts of England at the Queen's Coronation.

Apart from those, the household was increased by several mothers with daughters who went to the Swiss Girls' School to learn French and many other languages.

Alice had a house with many rooms, all of which were occupied by other guests, which is why Dorothy and Abigail had to stay at the hotel. During the course of the next week, Aunt Alice introduced the other guests staying with her. There was a large lounge where guests gathered to chat and this caused some amusement:

'We puzzled these guests very much just at first. We spoke Russian together, Abigail obviously knew no French or English, I spoke both. She was slightly older than myself but not a relation.'

While Dorothy was quite at home attending All Saints' Anglican Church where she was noticed and had been confirmed as a child, Abigail felt awkward, unfamiliar with, and unable to follow, the service.

Having visited the city before, Dorothy knew her way around town and frequently took Abigail with her when shopping. Abigail soon learned to speak a little French and English. The hotel became their home for two years and it wasn't long before the permanent guests living with Aunt Alice became good friends and knew all about Dorothy's affairs.

Abigail stayed with Dorothy until late March, 1931, when John arrived for three months of home leave. She then found a position with an elderly English family and some years later with an old, crippled Englishman, as nurse and travelling assistant when he went to England. By this time, Abigail was so proficient with the English language that she actually spoke at Speakers' Corner in Hyde Park on faith and the Bible. What she had to say was so very good and so much in earnest that no one ever sneered or was rude to her.

When she first joined Dorothy, she had to learn to speak some French so as to be able to shop for herself and to get around and of course, with Dorothy, she learnt English. Abigail had a tiny notebook in which she wrote down new words and sentences that she had come across each day. She had only two books: the Bible and Kipling's *Jungle Book*. Abigail and Dorothy translated the *Jungle Book* from English into Russian and then Abigail translated it into Swedish for herself.

As John had three months' home leave, he and Dorothy decided they would spend a month together in Lausanne before visiting his place of birth in Northern Ireland, which he had not seen since he first left as a young man. They would enjoy themselves, and when the time arrived, take a comfortable return journey to China.

~ FOURTEEN ~
Bab el-Mandeb, the Gateway of Lamentation

In late April, 1931, John and Dorothy left Lausanne and caught the train to Calais. They crossed the English Channel to Dover then on by Southern Railway to London, where they took the Great Western Railway train to Liverpool.

John wanted to visit his birthplace, a small village of only two or three houses in Ballyworphy, not far from Belfast in County Down. It was evening when they set sail and were fortunate to get a cabin on a ship crossing the Irish Sea. They had hoped to see the northernmost tip of the Isle of Man but it was too dark, though they could make out lights flickering in the distance.

The ship docked early in the morning at Belfast; after breakfast they disembarked, hired a car, and drove to Ballyworphy. John found the house where he had been born on 2nd April, 1885. The house was tiny, and derelict, as were the other houses. The only thing that John recognised was the kitchen hearth; the roof had collapsed, as had the upper floor where John's mother actually gave birth to her son. Weeds were growing through what remained of the floorboards. They spent a short time looking around what had once been a small but close community. The whole place was like a ghost village. Windblown trees, bare branches overhanging the broken roofs, looked as though some huge vulture had picked it clean leaving only the carcass behind.

John was not a sentimentalist; he briefly recalled the little education he had received as a child and, like so many of the Irish at that time, when he grew up was unable to get a job. At seventeen, he set sail for China, working his way on a tramp steamer to earn himself a little money to live on while he looked for employment. He started work with the Chinese Postal Service soon after he had disembarked.

In 1863, the Chinese Imperial Maritime Customs Service was placed under the direction of Sir Robert Hart. A man of genius, he and his staff became a dependable source of revenue and an agency for charting and lighting the coastal area of China; he also founded the Chinese Postal Service. Sir Robert Hart employed many of the poorly educated Irish who left their homes in Ireland to find work abroad. It was from the Chinese Imperial Maritime Customs Service that John had obtained his job in the Chinese Postal Service.

Dorothy and John returned to Liverpool. They spent a few days shopping for clothes they would need in China. Dorothy bought a blue chiffon evening dress and John a dark suit in case they were invited to any parties. These were luxuries; their other purchases were of a more practical nature suitable for the heat and dirt of Shanghai. When ready they made their way to the offices of the Blue Funnel Line and booked their passage to Shanghai on the steamship. On 20th June, 1931, they set sail for China.

The *Hector* was predominantly a passenger ship but did also carry cargo for the European market in China. One of four ships built by Cammell Laird, it carried 80 crew and 155 first class passengers; there was no second class. At the time they were regarded as the best looking ships of the day. The *Hector* had a length of 499 feet, breadth 62.3 feet and depth of 34.9 feet with twin screw, 4 single steam reduction turbines giving 15.5 knots; 15.5 knots is approximately 17.8mph. The journey would take an estimated four weeks.

The *Hector* passed through the Straits of Gibraltar on 24th June, docking at Marseilles two days later, but not before John, who was a poor sailor, had been violently sick as they passed through the Bay of Biscay. Although the *Hector* was not scheduled to berth long in Marseilles, both Dorothy and John went ashore for a couple of hours. John hoped to regain his land legs and to have a good meal to make up for what he had lost on the journey, and Dorothy bought face powder, hand lotion, lipstick and shampoo. Dorothy well knew how important this last item would be in Shanghai, where it was so difficult to keep hair clean.

Their next port of call was Port Said, (Bur Sa'id) where they arrived on

1st July. The outer harbour is formed by two breakwaters which protect the entrance to the Suez Canal. On the western arm breakwater there stands an enormous statue of Ferdinand de Lesseps, the French diplomat who was responsible for the construction of the Suez Canal, opened by the Khedive, Ismail Pasha, in 1869. On the same breakwater there is a lighthouse 174 feet high. Here in Port Said they decided to stay aboard ship.

Sailing through the Suez, they entered the Red Sea and were delighted to see so many varieties of multicoloured fish. On their left was the desert of El Hejaz El Yemen, and on the right, the sands of Egypt. Shortly afterwards, they passed through the towering cliffs of the Straits of Bab el-Mandeb, The Gateway of Lamentation, and Perim, the southernmost point of Yemen. It was now the 5th July; they noticed the sun reflecting off the salt pans to be seen on the sandy beaches of Aden. Crossing the Arabian Sea they arrived five days later at Colombo, the capital and largest seaport of Ceylon (Sri Lanka).

Colombo is warm, humid and low-lying; the Sinhalese came from the northwest and northeast India around 550 B.C. and began the civilisation of the Veddas. The Veddas, hunter-gatherers, were small in stature, a little over 5 feet; they lived in caves, hunting with bow and arrow and gathering wild plants and honey.

Now of course, coffee and tea plantations are found in the foothills of the mountain massif for which Ceylon is well known. Cinchona is also grown for the production of quinine. While here, Dorothy took the opportunity to buy a good supply of tea which they were in the habit of mixing with China tea to make a blend of their liking. They also took coffee beans which they would grind once home.

Leaving Colombo they saw no land until the evening of the third day when they saw the northern tip of Sumatra, Banda Aceh, in the distance. As they travelled due east, a craggy peak, shaped like a pyramid, slowly came into view towering out of the darkening sea; this was Gunung Jerai, which lies due north of Penang in the State of Kedah.

In the early hours of the morning they reached George Town on the Island of Penang. Some of the Europeans disembarked with their luggage which had to be brought up from the hold by crane. On waking Dorothy was surprised to see a massive mountain towering nearly 2,500 feet above. As their ship was not due to sail until the evening, Dorothy and John decided to explore the island. They took the hill railway and visited the Water Fall Botanic gardens 1,200 feet up the mountain which was spectacularly beautiful and surrounded by jungle. Dining at the E & O Hotel they went on to see St George's Church before returning to the ship. It was 15th July.

On the 17th July, *Hector* arrived at Singapore, just in time to have a late lunch at the Raffles Hotel, which in view of its worldwide reputation was very expensive; this came as no surprise. They decided on the Set Menu set out below: the dishes marked with * are those Dorothy and John chose.

APPETIZERS

Cream of sweet corn
crab ravioli and basil

Exotic mushroom salad
Asian celery and porcini potato wafer

Prawn 'cocktail'
Chilled avocado soup and Japanese mayonnaise

*Tempura chicken tenderloins
Wasabi mayonnaise and chilli jam

*Green leaf salad
snow peas, asparagus and kalamansi dressing

MAINS

Peking duck Caesar salad
Romaine lettuce, crumbed egg and garlic naan

*Golden snapper
spicy eggplant, lime and steamed rice

Sirloin steak
black peppered mushrooms and pomme purée

Stir-fried pasta
scallops and oyster sauce

*Drunken spring chicken supreme
creamed corn and smoked tomato coulis

DESSERT

Fresh fruit platter
Black and white sesame snaps
mango and home made vanilla ice cream
Selection of ice cream and sorbet
vanilla, lime and mandarin
*Jasmine valrhona chocolate Bavarian
exotic coconut pearl, kaffir citrus sorbet

SELECTION OF PREMIUM COFFEES AND TEAS

Lavender
Marigold
Lemon Verbena

*Ristretto
Espresso
*Macchiato
Cappuccino
Latté

After lunch, with coffee in one of the lounges, they decided to take a look around the island. Not far from the hotel stands St Andrew's Gothic Cathedral, built in 1862 and based on Netley Abbey in Hampshire. The spire rises high above the angsana trees that surround the cathedral. Painted white on the outside and with ceiling fans inside, Dorothy and

John found it pleasantly cool. On the other side of St Andrew's road, facing the Cathedral, is the Padang, like a park, where cricket is played. They would have liked to spend many more days in Singapore but the *Hector* could not wait. By now, they had been travelling for three weeks and were looking forward to reaching Shanghai, but still had a further 1,700 miles before Hong Kong.

Entering the South China Sea, they sailed past the southernmost point of Cambodia; the Khmer Empire ruled Cambodia from AD 802–AD 1432; it became a protectorate of France from 1863 to 1953, when it was known as the French colony of Indochina.

They followed the coastline of Anam (now Vietnam), past the island of Hainan, and on to Hong Kong, where they arrived on 23rd July.

When Dorothy and John sailed into Hong Kong it was, of course, still a British Crown colony. Passing by the Kowloon peninsular on the starboard side and Macau on its port side, the *Hector* docked in the harbour where most of the passengers, including John and Dorothy, disembarked.

Hector

They had arrived at the time of the southwest monsoon when it was very hot and humid so their clothes were soon soaked with perspiration. This is also the time for typhoons but fortunately, apart from the rain, they were not subjected to gale force winds during their short stay on the island.

Most of the shops and residential areas are situated around the harbour. They had come ashore ill-equipped for the torrential rain, so looked for and soon found, a shop that sold umbrellas. John bought an umbrella with a bright blue Horned Dragon, named Shen-Lung, the Spiritual Dragon, considered to be the most powerful of all dragons in Chinese mythology; it produces rain but is deaf. Dorothy's umbrella had a picture of a yellow dragon, Ti-Lung, the Earth Dragon, which controls water and rivers on the earth, and is supposed to emerge from water to bestow knowledge of writing. The Chinese dragon is the ultimate symbol of good fortune and is at the heart of Chinese mythology.

Glad to get out of the rain, Dorothy and John returned to the *Hector*, where they bathed and changed into clean clothes. Ahead of them lay their final destination: the commercial centre of China, Shanghai, an approximate 880 miles further north, which they hoped to reach in about 48 hours.

It was evening of the 24th July when the *Hector* weighed anchor and made its way up the coast of China passing through the Straits of Formosa (Taiwan). Although the sun had not quite risen, they were able to make out the lights of Quanzhou on the Chinese mainland, but it started to rain again and the sea became very rough. Although they had enjoyed relatively calm weather since passing through the Bay of Biscay, here on the East China Sea there was little swell but it was extremely choppy and the ship was thrown this way and that, with waves breaking over the bow as it plunged downwards into a trough before rising again. John was very sick and had to remain in bed.

They reached Shanghai on 27th July, 1931. The docks are situated on both sides of Whangpoo River (now Huangpu River), starting where the Whangpoo joins the Yangtze River. The *Hector* drew up to the dockside and they disembarked. John was thankful he was at last on terra firma.

Shanghai became a walled city in the sixteenth century and is one of the largest seaports in the world, and the nearest port to Japan. The

Yangtze River delta joins the East China Sea at Shanghai and irrigates the surrounding land for farming, and supplies the city with food, cotton and silk. In the 1930s there were between 30,000 and 60,000 foreign residents.

Dorothy now waited while John supervised the unloading of their meagre belongings from the hold of the ship and arranged for them to be taken to the Chinese Postal Commissioner's Residence, where they were to stay while in Shanghai. Holding only their hand luggage and umbrellas, John signalled to a bicycle rickshaw driver, who came and they both got in. The rickshaw was clean and had a serviceable hood which kept out most of the rain, and rain it did. The hood was garlanded with a pretty multicoloured, arrow-shaped fringe. The driver asked where he was supposed to go and John replied in perfect Chinese, much to the consternation of the driver. Dorothy thought she noticed a flicker of disappointment cross the rickshaw driver's face, and wondered, if he were carrying the customary Englishman, whether he had thought he might have been able to charge somewhat more; the usual practice in the East is to charge whatever you think you can get away with. Mounting his bicycle, the driver pushed down hard on the pedal to get moving, as John was not only tall but heavy. During the ride to their postal apartment, Dorothy watched fascinated by the knotted calf muscles of the driver as they strained up and down as he peddled, weaving his way between and around the motorised traffic and other rickshaws.

The Postal Office residence where they were to stay was near the district of Chapei. Chapei is the northern district of Shanghai and about 8 to10 miles from the centre. It is an industrial area and the Northern Railway Station is the terminus for trains to Woosung (now Wusong) and Nanking (now Nanjing). Known mostly for its heavy industries, Chapei was also famous for the production of brocaded silk. It is outside and separate from the international settlement where most foreign business hotels and businesses are situated.

~ FIFTEEN ~
Shanghai and Tientsin

A very tall Italian lady in a very short skirt
15th March 1932

Although John and Dorothy were not to stay in Shanghai for long, they were provided with a Postal Commissioner's Apartment in a hotel not far from the border of the district of Chapei within a few miles of the Main Post Office on the eastern side of the Woosong River.

On special occasions, John rode in processions with armed outriders wearing a ceremonial robe of blue silk, shot with gold thread; because of his stature, he was known as Mashensen, Sir Horse. (Philip Raitt, John's son-to-be, still has this ceremonial robe.)

Dorothy was not enamoured with Shanghai, so seldom went into the commercial centre. By now she was four months pregnant with her second child; at the age of thirty-one, she was deeply concerned, in view of her previous illness and the death of her firstborn at the age of eleven months. Dorothy was still subject to the occasional epileptic fit despite her medication and continued to suffer from this complaint for a further twenty-seven years.

Dorothy gave birth to Marjorie Eleanor Raitt Mclorn at home on Christmas Day, 1931. There were no complications.

Early in 1932, the Japanese commenced an undeclared war against China and by the end of February, they started to bomb Chapei: 'We could see the planes fly over then the bombs would fall and there would be an explosion followed by flames and smoke as Chapei was being destroyed. We moved the baby's crib out of the front bedroom into the passage where

Dorothy and Marjorie
Shanghai

the noise was less and where there was a little more safety from glass splinters should windows break.'

On the 1st March, the Chinese Army withdrew from Chapei leaving behind raging fires and a huge area of complete devastation. Within a few days the Japanese had occupied an area between Woosung Forts, situated near the mouth of the Whangpoo River where it joins the Yangtze River, north as far as Liu He and east of a line south to Nanziang and to the Soochow Creek, part of the Woosung River. This meant that Dorothy, John and their baby were now living in Japanese-held territory:

'The streets were noisy, with huge Japanese army trucks full of soldiers flaunting their power over the Chinese and we used to wonder how the

Chinese could remain so passive to all appearances. The trucks would turn aside for no one not for anything and heaven help those who got in the way.'

The occupiers represented greater Japan and everything else was of no importance. Even though the International Settlement was not yet occupied by the Japanese, there was a curfew from eight in the evening to six the following morning.

Dorothy had a friend who was matron of the British Hospital; the friend came off duty at eight o'clock in the morning and came to Dorothy's apartment to spend the day until she went on duty that evening. One morning, one of the Chinese hospital boys was away all night; in reply to her questions he told her that he was out after curfew

Dorothy and Children at Tientsin House

and had been arrested 'by a very tall Italian lady in a very short skirt'. This proved to have been a Scots soldier in a kilt with a strong brogue. 'This story sounded very funny at the time but at least it was original.'

The apartment hotel where Dorothy and John were living was just opposite the racecourse and this was where the *amah*, their nurse, used to take baby Marjorie for a walk in the pram. The racecourse was not open to locals and a policeman once stopped her from going in. *Amah* was very proud of her charge and lifting a corner of the blanket showed a tiny pink face and told him 'We belong to English baby.'

While in Shanghai, Dorothy and John would occasionally visit the really beautiful Jessfield Park (now Zhongshan Park) which was open only to non-Chinese, with the exception of course of the gardeners. Even though one had to pay to get in, the city must have spent a great deal of money to keep it looking so green and cool. Dorothy wondered what became of it after the Japanese occupation but never returned to find out. All the segregation of Europeans and 'natives' at that time was just a matter of course and the Europeans never thought about it.

In 1933, Dorothy and John moved to Tientsin, (now Tienjin). Here, the Chinese Commissioner's Postal Residence was a comfortable, two-storey house with a garden. The house was completely furnished and carpeted. Before they left Shanghai, Dorothy announced that she was pregnant again, and to celebrate the anticipated arrival of a new member of the family in Tientsin, she bought curtains in Shanghai; those for the baby's room had pictures of animals on a bright background.

Philip Raitt McLorn arrived on the 13th June, 1933, a strong bouncing baby. Even so, Dorothy was apprehensive as to whether her new son would survive and whether the birth would have an adverse effect on her occasional epileptic fits. She could not but reflect on the circumstances that surrounded her firstborn in such tragic and difficult times as the death of Governor Yang when living in Urumchi. They were thankful that all went well and the family were able to settle down comfortably in their new large house with its big garden.

The house was gated and walled with shards of glass embedded in the cement to stop thieves. The servants lived in small cottages within the grounds. Before the start of World War II, Ghurkha troops kept a close eye on the property and would chase away Russian gypsies. Each day, John would be taken to his office in a rickshaw pulled by the houseboy, who would then return and take the children to school.

In the summer they took a holiday in Pei de Hoa, a small quiet town on the edge of endless white beaches and an ocean of sea-blue and gentle white caps. This was their summer retreat from the stifling heat of the city. They travelled by train, accompanied by a maid/cook for Dorothy and an *amah* for the children. John would join them for a few days and catch up with old family friends. There were times, two or three times a year, when Pei de Hoa was hit by fierce monsoon storms. The sky would turn an eerie grey-black and the winds would blow at almost hurricane speeds. The rain pelted down on their beach house, cutting visibility to about six feet. On clear summer days the children spent much of their time following trails on donkeys. The forests were lush green, providing shade and a cool, inviting quiet. They would often stop to pick large white wild mushrooms, filling baskets, which would be carried by the maid and *amah*, and on the backs of donkeys. When they returned to the beach house, they spread the mushrooms out on sheets to dry in the sun.

Village craftsmen peddled delicate dolls, made of flour, baked and painted. The lady dolls were dressed in intricate and colourful finery. The males were dressed in battle armour, with black, scary beards and weapons. As the dolls often broke after the children played with them, the vendors replaced them almost every day.

One day, while they were relaxing on the verandah, a ship appeared, barely visible but easily spotted by a plume of black smoke. The battleship anchored when it got closer to the beach. Boatloads of American seamen jumped off the boats, yelling and screaming, having a wonderful time. After their journey in cramped quarters they wasted no time in setting up softball games and volleyball nets. As expected, the beach soon swarmed with vendors selling everything from souvenirs to food and drinks and of course, jewellery. Dressed in sparkling formal whites, the Captain and several good-looking (according to Dorothy) officers, came to their house bringing greetings from the US Navy. Soon the beer came out in ice-filled tubs. Champagne was chilling in the tubs as well and there was enough gin and tonic to sink the warship.

A few days later, after the American ship had departed, the telltale

Tientsin
Dorothy Raiit McLorn
In the Drawing Room, Summer 1934

black smoke appeared again on the horizon. This time it was a Japanese destroyer flying the 'Rising Sun' flag, anchored near the beach. Tenders hit the shore and Japanese sailors leapt out. They spent most of their time practicing martial arts in loincloths. Every one of them went swimming before returning to the ships. No good wishes this time and no vendors. This was to be the last of their peaceful days.

These were troubled times. The Japanese occupation of Manchuria had commenced in 1931 to the condemnation of America and Europe and as a result Japan left the League of Nations and continued to advance into Northern China.

It was not long before they reached Harbin, where Dorothy's parents were living. They found life most unpleasant, if not actually dangerous, for British Nationals. In 1935, Dorothy managed to persuaded her parents to leave Harbin, as she was again pregnant, and to join her and John in Tientsin. Life in Tientsin continued normally for the Mclorn family, though with Dorothy's parents, the house became somewhat cramped.

On 5th January, 1936, Dorothy gave birth to another daughter who was named Sally Dorothea Raitt Mclorn. Fortunately, there were no complications and Sally was born at home. With the new arrival the four-bed-roomed house became even more crowded. Initially, Sarah slept in her parents' bedroom until she was old enough to join the other two children in one room; there had to be a certain amount of shuffling of furniture to accommodate two beds, a cot, a large cupboard and chest of drawers.

Although Dorothy and her family were to remain in Tientsin for eight years, until the Japanese attacked Pearl Harbour in 1941, their life was to become one of worry and hardship.

On 17th July 1937, the Japanese took control of Tientsin in the space of one night; it had been very well planned. The day after the invasion of the city, they bombed many selected buildings: 'The planes,' Dorothy writes, 'would power dive, release their bombs, zoom up again and repeat the performance again and again until they ran out of bombs. Sad to say, there was no resistance.'

For a considerable time in Tientsin, Dorothy and her family had the barriers to contend with. This meant that people going in or out of certain areas had to produce their identity cards and inoculation and vaccination certificates. On occasions they had to submit to the searching of clothing or parcels. A good friend of theirs was stripped and searched. Undoubtedly, there were many other instances of a similar nature but people were too embarrassed to talk about them. This period of barriers was humiliating for foreigners, especially the British, whom the Japanese were determined to demean as much as possible.

The head office of the Chinese Post Office was across the river from the British, French and German Concessions in what was the old Russian Concession. John had arranged to move stamps and money into the sub-post offices in the British Concession; the Director General of the Service asked him formally to stay and 'keep the ship afloat' for as long as possible. Saving postal funds was a way of doing this. For a short while a Japanese official would either sit at a desk at John's office just to keep an eye on him, or someone would run in to use the telephone, or just come in and slam the door shut. This was supposed to distract and unnerve him. However, after a while, the Japanese gave up these tactics concluding that John was too popular with his staff and had far too much authority in Tientsin, so the family were transferred to Chefoo (Yen-T'ai), where they supposed that John would have less influence.

PART III

China
Internment

~ SIXTEEN ~
Chefoo

'This is my authority'
June 1942

The port that serves Tientsin is Tanggu and opens on to the Gulf of Chihli (now the Bohai Sea). From Tanggu, the coastline runs south and eventually arrives at the port of Chefoo, Yen T'ai, situated on the Yellow Sea in Shantung Province, a distance of about 300 miles. It is a deep water anchorage and an excellent, well-protected harbour not subject to silting. It is known for pongee silk cloth and tussore silk yarn. It has a long, dry summer and is noted for fruit growing, particularly grapes. Unfortunately, in the 1940s it was not served by rail and access was by mule trains, carts or motor trucks.

Early in 1941, Dorothy, John and their children moved into a Chinese postal house in Chefoo. On December 7th, 1941, without declaring war, Japan attacked Pearl Harbour. On the same day, John was arrested in the street on his way back to the office after lunch, and put in solitary confinement. He was accused of being a British spy.

Their coolie came home in tears, saying that John was so upset that he was almost crying. 'A big lorry,' he said, 'full of Japanese soldiers forced him to get into the truck and then they drove away.'

Later, on the same day as John's arrest, a Greek lady whom they knew came to say that all the British and American men had been arrested, but John was the first. They had been confined in the unheated summer hotel in Chefoo. The Greek lady, being neutral, was able to keep the families who had had their husbands arrested updated with the news of their menfolk.

The prisoners remained in the hotel for the next six weeks. Dorothy was allowed to visit John once a week to bring him food and any necessary clothing. For Dorothy, these weeks were a nightmare. She had to submit to having the house searched several times by the military who were looking for documents which would incriminate John as they were convinced that John, being British, was spying for his country; as he was a Chinese civil servant, they thought that he was also spying for the Chinese.

Having taken over all control of the Post Office, the Japanese stopped John's salary; lack of funds became a problem. The household at this time consisted of Dorothy's parents, the three children, the two *amahs*, their cook-boy, and Dorothy herself. They ate the cheapest foods: cornmeal bread and peanut oil. A friend who kept two pigs gave them a piece of bacon which lasted for a long while. Each member of the family was given a scrap from time to time as a treat. People were generally very kind. The Greek owner of a small grocery shop sent a message to say that Dorothy and her family could have anything they needed and pay only when John had returned home. For Dorothy's children, the house seemed empty without their father. All the luxuries of parties and outings ceased because of money and travel restrictions; their lives had changed for the worse and it had become a dark and empty period.

During the cold winter of 1941, Philip Raitt recalls what happened to bring them Christmas cheer and warmth:

'A gaily-dressed entourage arrived at our house singing carols, accompanied by instruments. The group was from our school the China Inland Mission School. They brought in a small, live Christmas tree, baskets of fruit, cakes and a feast of cold cuts and preserves. Gifts were loaded on to our outstretched arms. The servants looked elated and clapped in happiness and wonder. The group stayed for the afternoon and enjoyed cocoa and cake while we decorated the tree. I know that this was the best Christmas I ever had as a child.'

Dorothy and her family had only been living in the Chefoo postal house for eleven months when they were told they had to leave immediately. Fortunately, the China Inland Mission owned a good deal of property in the town and lent them one of their summer cottages; it was far from convenient and always bitterly cold in the winter when the water in the bedroom pitcher froze at night.

The cottage was not searched but on one occasion, as Dorothy was returning home, she met a Japanese civilian by the gate who demanded to search the house: 'I asked him to show me his documentary authority, he drew a revolver and said "this is my authority" so he and his companion came in and strolled about the rooms, chattered and laughed a bit and left.'

On another occasion, Dorothy had been to a tea party; her father came to escort her home. As they started down the hill, they came upon a wooden barrier across the path. Dorothy shouted for someone to move it, but nothing happened. They stood and waited; still nothing happened. In the end, Dorothy gave the log barring their way a shove, and down the hill it rolled with a lot of noise. A soldier appeared and shot at them a number of times. Dorothy heard the bullets whiz past her face but that was all. The officer in charge called Dorothy into the guardhouse and apologised most profusely when she complained at length in poor Chinese. He said it was a mistake on the part of a raw recruit.

The Japanese put out endless propaganda, which bore fruit in the behaviour of the young Chinese, but the British did not realise this until the war was over. This changed behaviour came as a shock when Dorothy and the family returned to Tientsin. She and John had always been fond of the Chinese, whether acquaintances, servants or others; they had treated the Chinese with the courtesy and respect due to good people and they had behaved in the same way toward Dorothy and her family: 'Because the Chinese is naturally courteous,' Dorothy says, 'no matter his position in life, I imagined that they actually liked us, until after the Japanese occupation. It was only after that, that I noticed they did not like us but that it had seemed they appreciated our trust and friendship.'

For some months there had been rumours that all the British and allied nationals would be interned. Several men sent their wives and children home.

Dorothy decided to stay behind with her husband and to remain in the Chinese Inland Mission summer cottage: 'I remember we spent that time in the cottage going for long walks and doing a great deal of mending.'

It was now imperative for John and Dorothy to reflect on what might happen at any moment: John could not work; were they doing the right thing by not returning to England with the children? It was in any event doubtful that they could get back, with war raging in Europe.

By now the Japanese had already overrun Malaya and the Dutch East Indies (Indonesia). On October 7th 1942, the US First Marine Division had landed, and were breaking out from the beachhead on Guadalcanal in the Pacific. The Battle of Cape Esperance was to start four days later. In the west, the British offensive 'Lightfoot', commenced at El Alamein on October 23rd. The further advance by the Japanese, who had already captured Burma, was halted by the commencement of the monsoon in May. By October, the tables were beginning to turn. Dorothy and John were out of touch with what was going on in the rest of the world; the only news they heard was the interminable propaganda broadcast by the Japanese which they did their best to ignore.

One fine October morning in 1942, a Japanese army truck drove up and their house was immediately overrun by armed soldiers. Dorothy and John were told that they, with their children, had to be at the Temple Mill Mission compound at noon. They were allowed to bring bedding, clothes, food and one piece of luggage per person: 'As we had made no preparations it was difficult to pack in a hurry and some belongings were left behind. The servants had to get out also and were in no state to help me.'

Dorothy took all the provisions she had stocked up that could be packed and also pots, pans, dishes and other kitchen equipment that could be carried: 'We also brought with us some ducks and geese that we had, and all this with a Japanese soldier in each room pointing his bayonet at one repeating, "quai, quai, hurry, hurry".' It was a scramble to hire enough rickshaws to transport all their things as their friends were doing the same: 'At last everything we could take with us was crammed on to the rickshaws.' The cook had managed to prepare hot food for them and had tied two or three pots of hot food to the axles of the rickshaws but they probably fell off; in any event, they disappeared.

When they reached the Temple Mill Mission compound, which comprised a number of detached houses, two schools and a hospital, families were placed in various houses where they were to live for the next eleven months. All the detached houses had been occupied by the Japanese at some time and wrecked.

As the families were not properly divided on the first night, fourteen people slept in one big room on the floor, on Dorothy's mattresses: 'There was too little water (which had to be pumped out of the ground), for washing and I seemed to be the only one with a jug and basin. We all shared the few tins of food we had with us and lights were out by eight o'clock at the request of an old couple who liked to sleep early.'

These uncomfortable conditions continued for about a week, after which the Japanese officer in charge, in collaboration with the committee who represented the internees, divided everyone among the rooms in the house. Dorothy, her children and the other British families had half, the other half was occupied by the China Inland Mission Girls' School, together with twenty or thirty girls, several teachers and their families. The headmistress was an old acquaintance of Dorothy from the days when she was at boarding school in Switzerland.

Dorothy's parents were placed with another group of people in a different compound and they were only able to see each other at Christmas. Rooms were allocated according to the size of the family. Dorothy, John and the children had a room twelve feet by twelve feet for the five of them as did the Murray family, also of five. Mr and Mrs Morrison, with only one boy, shared their room with the Anglican clergyman. The Rouses had a room for the four adults, while the two Roman Catholic priests shared a room with a Presbyterian Missionary. A Belgian lady had her three little daughters in her room.

There was a bathroom on the first floor for all these people but baths had to be shared as they could only be filled by heating pans of water one after the other and it took a long time. There was a huge kitchen in the basement. The housekeeping was shared among them all. The men pumped water and did the heavy work like stoking the furnace and carrying out the rubbish. The women cooked and the big girls of ten or older cleaned vegetables and helped generally. Camp food was basic: peanuts, bean-curd, cabbage and bread. Each family looked after their own room and laundry. Dorothy's job was to keep the bathroom clean and she also taught the little children reading and writing. The catering was done by a Chinese shop, the owner of which would be paid from a fund given to their committee by the Japanese. Dorothy remembers that it was four yen a day per person and they all ate well. As there was no dining room, food had to be eaten in the bedroom.

Philip recalls that on one occasion when a young boy of seven or eight, he was part of a Cub Scout pack. Their Cub mistress broke into the locked Anglican Church and pilfered every Cub and Scout uniform that she could carry, together with flags and banners. On her return she was mobbed by scores of young boys who were eager to try on their new regalia. In spite of the noise that ensued, the Japanese guards left them alone.

Philip used to while away countless hours copying a painting that his mother cherished. It was a watercolour of a house she once occupied. At some point one morning, a lanky, skinny young man stopped and admired his 'masterpiece': 'He suggested a couple of changes and said he would return the next day and give me some tips on drawing'. He became Philip's first art teacher. After their first meeting, the young man and Philip sketched together on several occasions. The name of Philip's new friend was Eric Liddle, the Scottish miler who refused to run in the Olympics on Sunday as it was against his religion. His story is beautifully told in the movie *The Chariots of Fire*. Subseqently, Eric became a missionary in China.

In the winter it became bitterly cold and everyone worried whether they would receive any more coal. Come the summer, the temperature could rise to 50°C so that all who were able slept out in the open. Early in 1943, the camp commandant handed over his responsibilities to Major Kosaka, who arranged for a sandpit to be brought into the camp for the children to play in.

At the end of eleven months, in September 1943, they were all moved from this really comfortable and homelike internment camp in Chefoo to a much larger one in Weihsien near Tsingtao (now Qingdao), about 120 miles south of Chefoo as the crow flies. The internees were taken around the Shantung Peninsula on a small ship where they were packed together so tightly that if anyone wanted to turn over at night the only way was to stand up, turn, and lie down facing the other way. It was crowded, hot, smelly and tedious. Rats were the size of small dogs and motion sickness was prevalent. There was no food and no water but most people were too seasick to want it until they arrived at Tsingtao, forty-eight hours later. They were not permitted to buy anything.

After a train journey of about one and a half hours, everyone had to get out and then they were taken by truck to the internment camp at Weihsien, where they were to live for the next three years. As the truck drove up to the entrance John, who not only spoke Chinese but wrote it also, noticed three Chinese characters over the large gate, he whispered into Dorothy's ear: 'Courtyard of the Happy Way'.

The camp was a former university and perfect for their three-year internment, but far too crowded for 1,800 prisoners of whom a third were children. It had a high wall and only one exit. An easily guarded gate was used by guards and merchants who brought in the bare necessities of life, including some food, paid for by the Red Cross.

The people already there turned out in force to welcome the new arrivals and lined the road calling greetings to friends they recognised as they filed in. Some days later, Dorothy heard that the internees already in the camp were disappointed when they noticed that the group Dorothy and her companions were with consisted mainly of the very old or feeble and young schoolchildren.

~ SEVENTEEN ~
Weihsien

'How can you read in the dark?'
June 1944

The Japanese opened the camp at Weihsien in March 1942. Dorothy, John and their children did not arrive there until a fine October morning in 1943. Their arrival coincided with the departure of 450 Roman Catholic Clergy and Nuns to Peking (Beijing) and the repatriation of 250 Americans and Canadians to New York. At the same time, there was an influx of some 400 teachers and children from the China Inland Mission. They had arrived at the tail end of the monsoon and the ground was one mass of mud. They had however, missed the heavy rains, when some walls collapsed, roofs leaked so that water poured into kitchens, dining rooms and many of the dormitories. To add to the misery, Dorothy could not help noticing that the accommodation consisted of row upon row of dismal-looking huts.

The weather during the summer was unbelievably hot and accompanied by blinding sandstorms from the Gobi Desert. Winters were freezing with fierce snowstorms. The small coal stoves were insufficient. Nightly, ice formed on the washbasins and buckets and had to be broken each morning. During the morning winter roll calls, Dorothy and her family wrapped themselves in blankets and huddled together for warmth. The Japanese guards wore greatcoats and knee-high leather boots, whilst the prisoners wrapped their feet in rags.

The grounds of the camp contained several large dormitories, some for schoolboys and single men, and some for schoolgirls and teachers. There were also rows of motel-like huts reserved for married couples with very young children. Dorothy, John and their youngest child, Sally, lived in one of these and their parents occupied a similar unit. Philip was placed in a male dormitory and Marjorie in another for schoolgirls. It was an easy walk for Philip and Marjorie to visit their parents and grandparents. The camp was huge, with few able-bodied men and women to cope with the hard work of feeding and managing fifteen hundred to two thousand people of all types: 'As in our little Chefoo compound,' Dorothy writes, 'every person had a job to do. The doctors and nurses worked in the hospital as aids, as did the girls. The young men 17 to 24 worked as cooks, the women who could sew, sewed. Some women did the hospital laundry; the men were bakers and yeast makers and vegetable cleaners. The more robust men hauled coal or vegetables from the gateway of the camp into the kitchens. The gates were always kept locked and guarded.'

A wall surrounded the camp with watchtowers at intervals and electrically charged barbed wire secured on top. Unfortunately, one of the students jumped up and grabbed a live wire; he was convulsed with shock and died, a dreadful sight for everyone. On another occasion, there was a great deal of excitement when two lads in their early twenties escaped. The rumour was that they joined up with a local Chinese warlord. Rations were cut immediately, guards were doubled and roll calls became more stringent. After about a month, everything went back to 'normal'.

For a time, John sliced bread and guarded the bakery against rats while keeping an eye on the stocks of coal and wood lest they be stolen and hoarded by fellow prisoners. It was surprising what a lot of stealing went on.

A sport the boys enjoyed was catching rats, using the old trick of an upside-down pail baited with food. Rats were trapped by pulling a string. They swapped rat-tails with guards, and kept the dining area free of flies by killing hundreds. These efforts were rewarded with tins of fish or corned beef, all with British or American labels. The internees ate in the mess halls at long tables sitting on benches. At meal times the food was doled out by the women on duty at the time, so much stew, gravy, a slice of bread and a mug of tea. The bread was often sour with weevils here and there. If you accidentally ate one they added to the sour taste but usually everyone fished them out. The meat was frequently so high that it was noticeable some distance away even if a lot of pepper had been added. After the meal, the dishes were given a wash of a kind in a big jar of hot water.

In the camp, plumbing was non-existent. Every morning there was a slop parade and containers would be emptied into a round hole about twelve feet in diameter, the smell from which was disgusting. As it was not fenced off in any way and was situated where the main paths crossed, it was a wonder that only one small child fell in who for ever afterwards bore the name 'Cesspool Dannie'. The latrines around the camp were emptied daily by Chinese coolies, the precious night soil being taken away and used as manure on the fields. These coolies came and went past the guards at the gate who never gave them a second look. They were dirty, humble, and doing a filthy, smelly job.

Dorothy remembers an occasion when one of the coolies, as he came in at the gate, threw down a cigarette stub which was promptly snatched up by a priest who happened to be loafing about nearby, to the sneering amusement of the guards: 'A European so crazy for a cigarette that he can pick one up that a dirty coolie threw away.'

Dorothy believed that this seizure of cigarette stubs happened every now and then. What the Japanese guards did not discover was that the 'cigarette' was a rolled-up scrap of paper with minute writing giving news of the war, sent by a priest from Eire who had an illicit radio outside the wall from which he listened to the latest news. Some time after Dorothy and her family had been freed and came to Canada she learnt that these news items were posted on the wall of the men's washroom, but no one ever mentioned it. The Japanese Commandant assured the committee representing the internees that they would be informed as soon as there was a victory for either side, but he never offered the information. Initially, all prisoners lived on rumours but eventually gave up listening to them altogether.

The food at Weihsien camp did not compare with the food at Chefoo, as it was often stale or even rotten. It was not altogether surprising as the Japanese bought all the stores and food themselves, which, Dorothy presumed, was brought by truck to the camp gates from where the 'robust' men hauled them to the kitchens on little carts. The Japanese in charge never interfered with the running of the camp. Their instructions and orders were delivered through the discipline committee, of three British and two Americans. The guards were only seen at roll call twice daily and on the watchtowers.

Dorothy, John and their youngest child, Sally, who was then six, lived in room 13/8, one of the ten by twelve feet former students' rooms. This whole compound had been a college run by the US Missionary Society. Their other two children, Marjorie and Philip, were in room 61/9 in the attic of the hospital building, with other Chefoo schoolchildren, where they all slept, were schooled and played when the weather was too bad to go out. They just had a mattress each to sit and to sleep on. The whole camp was infested with bedbugs and sleep, even for a child, was constantly being broken by these pests. Everyone did their best to keep them at bay but never succeeded in getting rid of them altogether. Considering the poor food, the cold in winter when everything froze, and the extreme heat in the summer which brought forth mosquitoes, even more bedbugs and rats, nearly everyone had reasonable health.

There was always the threat of malaria. Mosquito nets were a necessity and were dropped over the beds at dusk and rolled up in the morning. Bugs and ticks hid in the crevices and corners of the nets and bedding. The morning ritual was to squash and eliminate these pests. Ticks were ferocious, and attached themselves to bare skin by sucking blood. Dorothy used to get rid of them with a lit cigarette. Unfortunately, John suffered from malaria and often had to be carried to the hospital by anyone kind and strong enough to use a stretcher. The food in the hospital was better than that in the kitchen mess halls, but meagre. There were several good doctors from Peking, Chefoo and Tientsin. Twenty-seven babies were born in camp.

Children got four ounces of milk a day until their seventh birthday; newly born babies and their mothers got orange juice as well as milk. Before lunch and dinner started everyone queued up stoically, in an orderly fashion. Any child who could be persuaded to take it was given a teaspoon of calcium made of hand-crushed eggshells. The lady serving would give each child a crust of bread to help force the eggshells down their throat. Those who dared to take it choked badly as it tasted disgusting. Enough protein was another problem for children. They seemed to be able to obtain lots of chicken and sometimes pork from local farmers, but when Philip enquired what they were actually eating Dorothy would wink and make the whinny sound of a horse. Bread pudding was the camp 'favourite'. It was described in many ways and was doled out at just about every meal. The recipe consisted of taking stale bread, cutting off the telltale rat's teeth marks and mouldy bits, and soaking it in water overnight. The mixture was then heated and served. If a few raisins were added it became bread pudding or, if baked, it became scones or muffins. Dorothy and John had no rats in their room, only tiny mice which Dorothy hated to catch in their homemade trap; but there were rats in the bread room and they would gnaw a hole right through rows of loaves of bread from one narrow end to the other. Now and then they were given millet or cornmeal or soya bean gruel. If anyone was ill, they got the best care possible.

Clothes and shoes were a problem for all, but especially shoes for the growing children, so they were passed along the line from one to another until they eventually fell to pieces. Shoes that were too small had the toe caps cut out so they did for a while longer. The paths were mostly covered in cinder and painful to walk on in bare feet but the bigger children got used to it. They all did their best to wear shoes to church services but this was not always possible. The services were held on Sunday in the assembly hall by each denomination in turn, from early morning to dusk, and were well attended.

In camp there was supposed to be electricity but frequently it faded out, so most people made candles from scraps of candle wax or would use peanut oil lamps, which gave a tiny light, not bright enough to read by but better than nothing. Each room had a stove which burned 'coal balls' in the winter. These balls were made by mixing a certain amount of coal dust, clay and water to a stiff paste, rolling them into neat balls as big as a large egg, which were either dried in the summer sun or frozen in winter, then brought inside and stacked in each room until required.

The bed which Dorothy shared with her daughter was raised by five bricks beneath each leg, thus making room for coal, kindling wood, a box or two and the basin, jug and water pail. When they first arrived in camp, John asked for boards to make shelves but was told he had to scrounge for anything he needed. So they both walked with eyes on the ground looking for anything that could be put to use. On one occasion Dorothy found a piece of wire from which she made herself a pair of hair pins. Bits of paper, nails, wood shavings were all salvaged. The Anglican Clergy were all competent carpenters since in peacetime they were frequently given a poor parish where the locals did not know how to use wood, so the clergymen would teach them. Among the clergy was Eric Liddell, the Olympic 400 metre champion in 1924 in Paris. He had taught at the Anglo-Chinese School in Tientsin, married in March 1934 and had three daughters who together with his wife he sent to Canada in 1941 to avoid capture by the Japanese. Regrettably he died on 21st February 1945 of a brain tumour and typhoid while in Weihsien where he spent four years and was buried outside the gates of the Camp. He was a hero and an inspiration to all the camp members.

There was a lot for the clergy to do in the camp. Mending roofs, floors, doors and windows, making benches and other tasks. One of the men from the Chinese Inland Mission was a good cobbler so was kept extremely busy. Cigarettes were used as currency and everyone was issued a certain number per person and if anyone wanted more then they had to be willing to earn them by doing a lot of extra jobs. Those who did not smoke, like the Missionaries, traded their cigarettes for extra food which they gave to the children. The canteens stocked the occasional potato or onion, peanut oil and peanuts. Cabbage, turnips, carrots and an evil-like grain called *gaug liang,* were sometimes available from local farmers. Flour was delivered regularly and Red Cross parcels and 'Care Packages' from German and Italian friends who stayed out of the conflict with Japan, supplemented their diet. Dried apricots or persimmons and soap were issued to everyone, one cake of white soap for laundry and one of pink to wash with per person per month.

No one had time to be bored after the daily chores were done at home as there was always something happening: glee clubs, lectures, plays, concerts, street dances and language study, business classes or games or walks. The children had Cubs, Scouts, Brownies and Guides after school. School classes were held wherever convenient. In spite of a great shortage of writing material, students passed the Oxford and Cambridge Matric Exams satisfactorily. The papers were based on exams of several years earlier and were actually forwarded through the Japanese officials to the proper destination, as were the results. There was both an adult and a children's library well run by volunteers. Children both young and old spent much of their free time running treasure hunts. Secret messages with clues were hidden all over the camp. Teams found and decoded the messages, dashing on to the next clue. Children also had daily communal activities: forming briquettes, cooking, pumping water, cleaning latrines and washing laundry. Laundry could not be hung out to dry if it could be seen from beyond the walls in case they were sending out signals. On a few occasions, young officers in sportswear would 'coach' them in Ju Jitsu. They were polite and gentle.

Apart from the watchtowers and electrified barbed wire, the camp was carefully guarded by armed patrols, searchlights and Alsatian dogs, trained to kill. Most of the guards were militia or retired policemen. No signs of cruelty were shown. Young children of all ages raced over the camp playing hide-and-seek, hunting for treasure and, of course, playing Cowboys and Indians.

There must have been some system for the inmates of the camp to obtain money; Dorothy assumes people sold gold cufflinks or tiepins or any such things of value, whatever they had which the Chinese were prepared to buy. This trading was strictly forbidden by the Japanese and if discovered the punishment would be severe.

Bartering required great patience, a knowledge of Chinese and enormous cheek. All these talents were present in the person of a certain Father Scanlan, an Australian Trappist Monk, who became a legend in the camp. Father Scanlan himself composed rhymes and songs about his exploits. He could not bear to see little children in the camp with too little nourishing food to eat and traded with the Chinese peasants over the wall to improve their lot. This he did in an organised way; he moved his camp bed out of his room into the opening near the wall.

One night when he had just collected some food from the Chinese and was waiting for an opportunity to hand it over to his friends in camp, the Japanese sentry passed and asked why he was sitting there. 'I am reading my prayer book.'

'How can you read in the dark?'

Father Scanlan replied that if he tilted the book toward the sky he could see by the shape of the page where he was in his prayers and could go on from there.

The sentry said 'You are a queer teacher,' and went away. However, he was caught with the food eventually and taken away and locked up in the guardhouse in the Japanese end of the compound. Father Scanlan made a point of praying and singing hymns and psalms very loudly at all hours of the night. When the guards objected, he replied that he was a priest and his duty was to pray and praise God by day and night. He had been sentenced to several weeks of solitary confinement, but the noise he made was more than the Commandant could bear and in ten days, he was released. The whole camp rejoiced and thronged about him as he was led to his quarters by the Salvation Army Band.

One of the best things about the camp community was a great spirit of friendliness and co-operation. Nationality, race, creed or class made little difference: 'We all helped each other when we could, whether it was pumping or carrying pails of water, helping with the wash, mending or lending the one and only food grinder for the peanut butter.' Dorothy's job was helping in the 'Elephant Bell' shop, so-called because it was a cross between a White Elephant and a Camel Bell Antique Shop where clothes or anything else could be exchanged for goods or cash. It was like a rummage sale but less exciting, held each Saturday morning. Baby clothes used to come back again and again as one baby outgrew the things and another became big enough to wear them. No one ironed their clothes except perhaps for a wedding, of which there were two or three. Clothes were drip-dried in the sun or in the rooms near to the stoves. Wooden washtubs could be bought in the canteen and Dorothy did her washing outside even in cold weather. Hot water had to be carried from quite a distance, one pail per family, and rationed a bucket a day.

There was a variety of nationalities imprisoned in Weihsien: British, Americans, a few Russian and a few Chinese who had British or American passports, and a smattering of French, Australian, New Zealanders and everyone from the C.I.M. School: students, teachers, some missionaries and support staff. Their luckiest catch of all was an American Dance band made up of African American musicians from the Tientsin Country Club. Concerts were held in which everyone who had played in an orchestra took part. Several of the Roman Catholic nuns were violinists, the Anglican Bishop played the cello, there were several good pianists and the Salvation Army Brass Band and the jazz orchestra from the Peking Hotel for dancing. There were good voices too, many trained, others just liked to sing. At Christmas and Easter there were Cantatas, and for the children a pantomime. *Dick Whittington* was staged during the holidays and the nuns put on a pageant in which every single child in camp was given a part as an angel, a shepherd or one of the crowd. If the electricity failed for any performance people were asked to bring peanut-oil lamps; a large number of these 'footlights' helped to lighten the gloom if not to light the stage. Costumes were a problem, but an amusing one. To gain entry everyone had to bring something: a coal briquette, sugar, beans, rice, possibly tinned food, and always a candle or oil-lamp to light the stage.

For the average, healthy family, life in camp was varied by all these many means. But for the very old or sick, existence was truly dreadful. One sickly old Indian gentleman, Mr Talati, who owned apartment houses, a hotel and some silk shops, was offered a chance to leave camp if he renounced his British citizenship. He replied that he had become wealthy under the British and he certainly was not going to change at this point.

After Italy decided to join the allies, the Italian population of North China were taken into internment camps; the Japanese segregated them in case the other inmates abused them. What in fact happened when the Italians were put into Weihsien camp was that some of the Roman Catholic priests went to all the houses to borrow the things that the new arrivals would need: basins, jugs, dishes, spoons and knives, pots and pans. Everyone lent what they could and though the Italians kept to themselves there was never any trouble in the camp; in fact, people went out of their way to make life easier for them.

During the internment, Weihsien was a self-governed camp under the scrutiny of the Japanese captors. Committees were formed to organize every aspect of prison life. Several camp-appointed men who reported directly to the Japanese commandant, headed these committees. They determined the rules of camp life and meted out punishment for those who disobeyed the rules. Most prisoners were willing to do their part and look after health issues: food, hygiene, rations, kitchens, hospital matters, sanitation, education, social events and activities. The Japanese wanted nothing to do with running the camp and were mainly concerned with roll call – which went on endlessly – to determine that no one had escaped. Nevertheless, rumours and messages about the progress of the war were brought to them in many ways such as the 'bamboo radio', reports hidden in food supplies brought into the camp by coolies, and 'honey dippers' who slipped tiny notes on silk rolled into prophylactics to the black marketeers; these messages had been hidden in every orifice.

The messages did not fill the gap of reliable news about what was happening in the rest of the world. What little other news reached the prisoners mostly came in the form of Japanese propaganda, which no one believed.

In 1944, after the heat of the summer, they were back again to monsoon weather of foul-smelling, slippery mud and by the end of the year another freezing winter. The food shortage got worse. Prisoners suffered illnesses, including typhoid, scarlet fever and malaria. Weight loss was dramatic and most adults weighed under one hundred pounds. Children were not developing properly. When babies' teeth appeared, they grew in without enamel and young girls did not menstruate. People were starving and malnourished and thievery increased, so additional guards were employed. All suffered alike. Clothes were worn-out and threadbare, winter clothing no longer kept out the freezing cold. Some of the women made men's pants out of blankets, which didn't last long.

Outside the camp, a hidden radio in the town was broadcasting news of the progress of the war. These reports were given to Father Scanlon. Stories and rumours were rampant throughout the camp. It was rumoured that the war was coming to an end and they learned that their gaolers had been given orders to shoot all prisoners if the war did not end in the Japanese favour. As the 40s rolled by, the rumours of allied victories were on more and more lips. The guards appeared sullen. Then in 1945 the story of A-bombs filtered into the camp.

~ EIGHTEEN ~
Liberty at last

We got plenty to eat
August 1945

In January 1945, it was bitterly cold; the snow lay on the ground and the ground was like iron. Out of nowhere, American Red Cross parcels arrived on donkey carts. Each parcel was huge and contained mainly food. Each family was allowed one parcel and any that remained were passed to other camps. These parcels had to last each family into spring and beyond.

By May of 1945, the internees knew that the war in Europe was over and by June everyone was becoming increasingly nervous as they sensed the Japanese would take the law into their own hands and kill them all before relief was at hand.

On August 6th, 1945, the first atomic bomb was dropped on Hiroshima. Three days later a further atomic bomb was dropped on Nagasaki but it was not until August 17th that the inmates of Weihsien heard of these raids.

On Wednesday August 15th, 1945, armistice was announced. The war was officially over but the Weihsien internees did not receive confirmation until two days later. On a lovely summer's morning a USA B-29 Flying Fortress crisscrossed the camp several times. On each run, leaflets in English and Japanese were dropped, telling them that the war was over and that the Japanese guards were staying to protect them from marauding Chinese warlords. Prisoners streamed out of their quarters, shouting, laughing, crying and hugging each other.

Dorothy was at the White Elephant with the door open when she suddenly noticed seven red and white and green parachutes slowly floating down:

'We all rushed into the street and the small boys ran to the gates which were wide open and not a guard in sight. We ran into wasteland where the parachutists were landing; an American armed soldier stood up from behind a haystack and approached. He was followed by five or six more as they replaced their revolvers in the holsters.'

The American soldiers were prepared to shoot if the Japanese attacked them; they were carried shoulder high back to the camp where the Japanese commandant surrendered.

'We were informed that the war was over; Germany, Japan and their allies had surrendered.' Dorothy had heard rumours to this effect but it seemed to be too good to be true so she hadn't believed them. But now the Americans were there it changed everything. No one knew what to do; everyone talked, laughed or cried, as rules or regulations all went by the board.

Almost immediately, cartloads of food of all description were being delivered. It was at first shared out slowly because the internees were suffering from malnutrition and had to be careful of what they ate to avoid being sick. As they grew stronger, they were given more.

Dorothy was ecstatic: 'We got plenty to eat, as many eggs as we wanted, not just one egg per person a week.' There was also chewing gum, chocolate bars, sports equipment, C-rations and even medical supplies.

Meanwhile, their living quarters were made more comfortable and pleasant. Reels of current films and projectors were brought in and a makeshift radio station using loudspeakers brought music throughout the camp. The older generation put on their finest shirts and skirts and danced the nights away with beer, bourbon and cigarettes, all courtesy of the USA. There was enough sports equipment for four baseball teams which brought hours of enjoyment.

Because the internees had little or no idea as to how the war had progressed, the American soldiers gave them all a history lesson on the war, finishing with an account of the two atomic bombs dropped on Hiroshima and Nagasaki, which more than anything else contributed to the ultimate surrender of the Japanese.

John became the hero of the day when he made his way into town and, using his fluent Mandarin, was able to bargain for fresh fruit. He sold his last pair of gold cufflinks and all the family cheered when he brought back a luscious watermelon.

In September, a British colonel visited the camp to interview all British personnel. It was a sad story for many of the internees. All their businesses had been destroyed in the fighting, Chiang Kai-shek's government was in power and all foreigners were now subject to Chinese law. He suggested that they should as soon as possible return to Britain or move to other Commonwealth countries. For those who had been born and brought up in China, this briefing came as a dreadful shock. They literally had to start their lives again from scratch. It took about three weeks for things to calm down and life became more normal. Eventually steps were taken to return home all who had been in the camp. John's brother Dan and his wife Olive, who had been interned in Shanghai, took the first opportunity to fly home to Missouri.

It was toward the end of the year before Dorothy, John and their children eventually left the internment camp. The date of their departure kept being postponed, but the fact that they would leave eventually made their days more bearable. The place was being dismantled and the prisoners got much more to eat – eggs galore and many tinned foods provided by the Americans – so that in that sense, life was easier. When the time arrived they left in groups: the Peking-British, Tientsin-British, Tsingtao-British, the Americans and so on. All their luggage, such as it was, had been packed and forwarded days before so they had no bedding, no change of clothes and few eating utensils. They slept on the bare floors with a sweater each, which they used as a pillow or as a cover if they felt chilly.

The big gates of the internment camp were now open and although many prisoners went for walks to the town, Dorothy never did. When the time came for her and the family to leave she had an odd feeling as they passed through the gates after a total of four years of internment by the Japanese. A feeling that the life she had known had come to an end and they all would have to start again. A new life into a blank unknown.

Dorothy remembers that they were driven out in an American truck and then flown out on a Boeing 29 Superfortress to an airport near

Tientsin and finally on another truck into Tientsin itself. Here the family were met by kind smiles and greetings of the Chinese peasants and others as they drove to the Tientsin Club to be registered and told where they would live and fed until they had decided to make their own arrangements.

Dorothy's parents continued on to Lausanne, where they lived for the rest of their lives.

John not only lost his job of twenty years but also his pension and life savings. He got a position with the United Nations Relief Rehabilitation Association, guarding cattle and food, as it was unloaded from Victory ships.

Dorothy and the family were billeted in the house of the manager of the Standard Oil Company, as were several other people. Their room contained a number of camp cots with two US Navy blankets each: 'We had a pretty green bathroom – plumbing and all!! Having been used to living in one little room for three years, I could not settle down anywhere but in one room. All our meals were provided (I wonder now – by whom?) in the US Marine's Mess Hall and were splendid.'

The only snag was that it took forty-five minutes to walk each way from where they lived. Money was very scarce but Dorothy did manage to get a pair of navy-blue socks and some running shoes, as her other shoes were worn out.

The Dan McLorns had also been released from camp and were back in Shanghai. Dorothy never learnt of their experiences while interned. Dan McLorn sent Dorothy and the family a number of things he thought they might need, as all the family possessions had been looted and other people were using the postal furniture and household equipment:

'Thus, we got volumes of the *Book of Knowledge* for the children, a large set of table flatware and an old mink jacket for me that belonged to an old dinner-jacket suit which I had made into a suit for myself, some brown velvet draperies which were made into a garment for one of the girls, and so on.'

The Chinese shopkeepers charged absurdly low prices so they existed for the time being. When the family left the Standard Oil Company house, they lived in a flat above the Victoria Road Post Office and shortly after, moved to another flat in the ex-German Concession. Here they lived in two large rooms and a kitchen upstairs; a Chinese man lived downstairs with his family and friends. All their luncheons were had at the Russian Club, clean wholesome, adequate and dull. For dinners and special occasions they were invited to the Padeshankos'.

Dorothy was anxious to track down Takaloi Amah, so-named as she had owned a lighting shop on that road. She found her in the deserted Postmaster's house which had been the family home in Tientsin before the war. It was a happy and cheerful reunion. She was wealthy and lent John much-needed funds until he got settled. She had buried all the family silverware and precious objects before the Japanese could take them and these she dug up and gave to Dorothy and John, who were destitute. Amah had used the house as a red-light destination for Japanese officers. The prostitutes were called 'singsong girls'. She had always remained faithful to the family and did what she could to survive the Japanese occupation.

They hired a cook who had been with a German family for years and came to join Dorothy when the Germans could no longer afford to keep him. After Dorothy and the family left for Canada he returned to the German people. He felt that they needed him although they could hardly pay him at all. He spoke no English and only a few words of German but between them, they understood each other. His fondest memories seemed to have been of the time he went to France during the First World War in the Chinese labour corps. The Sergeant Major was his hero, a stern but fair person whom he admired immensely. The food they were given, he thought marvellous, so delicious and plentiful. The British soldiers' amusements, sports, games and practical jokes made him laugh as he told Dorothy about them – his memories of thirty years ago. He begged Dorothy to take him to Canada but they had to refuse; he would have been too homesick and lonely without his wife and family. In any event, Dorothy had no idea what it would be like in Canada as she had never been there before, or when or how they would settle down eventually. He was too old to learn new ways but a nice faithful person.

While Dorothy and her family lived in Chekiang Lane, the children attended school. Philip was a boarder at the Roman Catholic St Louis College, run by Franciscan Brothers. The school distilled brandy and cognac which they sold throughout the community. Philip had a difficult time since he hadn't attended regular classes for four years and the availability of brandy and cognac didn't help.

Sally was a boarder at St Joseph's Girls' School, run by sisters, while Marjorie attended as a day girl. It was a long and unpleasant walk for Marjorie, particularly as the Chinese youth, trained by the Japanese to scorn white people, used to make rude remarks, spit on the schoolchildren and blow their noses on them.

Dorothy and her children remained in Tientsin for two years after the end of the war. It took John months to get together enough money for a berth on the Liberty Ship – the USS Boulder *Victory* – carrying cattle, leaving for San Francisco where it docked in April 1947.

From San Francisco, they took various trains to St Thomas in Ontario, Canada where John's uncles were living. John joined them two years later in 1949 after he had finished his contract with the Chinese Postal Service and fleeing the Communist Regime.

John McLorn died in December 1959, in Canada.

Dorothy McLorn had a stroke in 1987 from which she never regained consciousness and died at the age of 90 in 1990, also in Canada.

London, Ontario
Dorothy McLorn 1986

Szsaigen, Goodbye'

In old age I live anew, the past unrolls
before me. Did it in years long vanished
sweep along, full of events, and troubled like
the deep ? Now it is hushed and tranquil.
Few the faces which memory saved for me, and few
The words which have come down to me – the
rest has perished, never to return.
Alexandr Pushkin, *Boris Godunov*

Acknowledgements

I would like to thank:

John Westwood – an authority on Russian Railways of the early 20th Century.

Ruth Barriskill, Guildhall, Printed Books Department – greatly assisted me in the identification of ships of the Blue Funnel Line.

Professor Phillip Hanson of the University of Birmingham, who advised me on sources of information on life in St Petersburg during the early 20th century.

Mr Ron Bridges, Chairman of the Association of British Civilian Internees Far East Region from May 2001 and who was himself interned in Weihsien, gave me detailed information of where the McLorn family were housed in Weihsien.

Mr Stuart Thompson, School of History, University of Nottingham, supplied me with various sources of information in regard to life in St Petersburg during the early 1900s.

Sonia Ribeiro, Literary Consultant and Editor, who has patiently and painstakingly guided me with my manuscript and which, without her help, would never have been published.

Margaret Easton of the North Yorkshire County Council Library at Boroughbridge who so helpfully obtained copies of the many books I required for research.

CPSIA information can be obtained at www.ICGtesting.com
Printed in the USA
LVOW081743140911

246286LV00002B/27/P

9 781848 761322